Study Skills and Strategies

for Students in
High School

Third Edition

Charles T. Mangrum II, Ed.D.
Stephen S. Strichart, Ph.D.

Mangrum-Strichart Learning Resources
Loveland, Colorado

www.mangrum-strichart.com

Copyright © 2011 by Mangrum-Strichart Learning Resources
2634 Glendale Drive
Loveland, CO 80538
Internet: www.mangrum-strichart.com
Authors: Charles T. Mangrum II
           Stephen S. Strichart

All rights reserved. No part of the material protected by this copyright notice may be reproduced or utilized in any form or by any means, electronic or mechanical including photocopying, recording, or by any information storage and retrieval system, without written permission from the copyright owner. The reproducible masters contained within may be reproduced for use with this book, provided such reproductions bear copyright notice, but may not be reproduced in any other form for any other purpose without written permission from the copyright owner.
ISBN 978-0-9797723-4-4
Printed in the United States of America

Contents

Unit 1 — Study Time, Place, Habits, and Goals 1

    Activity 1-1 Managing Study Time 2
    Activity 1-2 Monthly Planner 3
    Activity 1-3 Practice Preparing a Monthly Planner 5
    Activity 1-4 Weekly Planner 8
    Activity 1-5 Practice Preparing a Weekly Planner 10
    Activity 1-6 Daily Planner 13
    Activity 1-7 Practice Preparing a Daily Planner 15
    Activity 1-8 My Study Habits 18
    Activity 1-9 Improving My Study Habits 21
    Activity 1-10 My Study Place 22
    Activity 1-11 Improving My Study Place 24
    Activity 1-12 Setting Goals 25
    Activity 1-13 Practice Setting Goals 27
    Activity 1-14 What I Have Learned 28

Unit 2 — Interpreting and Creating Visual Aids 31

    Activity 2-1 Pictograph 32
    Activity 2-2 Create a Pictograph 34
    Activity 2-3 Pie Graph 36
    Activity 2-4 Create a Pie Graph 38
    Activity 2-5 Vertical Bar Graph 40
    Activity 2-6 Create a Vertical Bar Graph 42
    Activity 2-7 Horizontal Bar Graph 44
    Activity 2-8 Create a Horizontal Bar Graph 46
    Activity 2-9 Line Graph 48
    Activity 2-10 Create a Line Graph 50
    Activity 2-11 Table 52
    Activity 2-12 Create a Table 54
    Activity 2-13 Timeline 57
    Activity 2-14 Create a Timeline 59

Contents

    Activity 2-15 Diagram... 61
    Activity 2-16 Political Map.. 63
    Activity 2-17 What I Have Learned... 65

Unit 3 — Reading and Taking Notes from Textbooks 67
    Activity 3-1 Learning About the PQRW Strategy................................ 68
    Activity 3-2 The Preview Step 70
    Activity 3-3 The Question, Read, and Write Steps 79
    Activity 3-4 Practice Using PQRW... 85
    Activity 3-5 Practice Using PQRW... 96
    Activity 3-6 Practice Using PQRW... 111
    Activity 3-7 What I Have Learned... 122

Unit 4 — Taking Notes in Class 125
    Activity 4-1 Identifying Signal Words and Statements 126
    Activity 4-2 Using the Fewest Words... 128
    Activity 4-3 Using Common Abbreviations for Words 129
    Activity 4-4 Using Your Own Abbreviations for Words 130
    Activity 4-5 Using Abbreviations for Terms..................................... 131
    Activity 4-6 Using Symbols for Words or Terms 132
    Activity 4-7 A Two-Column Notetaking Format................................. 133
    Activity 4-8 Taking First Notes... 136
    Activity 4-9 Rewriting First Notes 139
    Activity 4-10 Creating a Graphic Organizer for Rewritten Notes 141
    Activity 4-11 Recognizing Other Lecture Styles 142
    Activity 4-12 What I Have Learned... 149

Unit 5 — Using Reference Sources 151
    Activity 5-1 The Internet... 152
    Activity 5-2 Dictionary 154
    Activity 5-3 Choosing the Correct Meaning 157
    Activity 5-4 Thesaurus 158
    Activity 5-5 Practice Using a Thesaurus 160
    Activity 5-6 Choosing the Correct Synonym.................................... 161
    Activity 5-7 Encyclopedia... 162
    Activity 5-8 Almanac... 164
    Activity 5-9 Statistical Abstract of the United States 166
    Activity 5-10 Atlas 168
    Activity 5-11 Occupational Outlook Handbook................................. 170
    Activity 5-12 What I Have Learned... 172

Contents

Unit 6 — Remembering Information ... 175
- Activity 6-1 Repetition ... 176
- Activity 6-2 Visualization ... 178
- Activity 6-3 Categorization ... 181
- Activity 6-4 Rhyme ... 183
- Activity 6-5 Acronym ... 186
- Activity 6-6 Acronymic Sentence ... 188
- Activity 6-7 Pegwords ... 191
- Activity 6-8 Keyword ... 194
- Activity 6-9 Loci Strategy ... 196
- Activity 6-10 What I Have Learned ... 203

Unit 7 — Graphic Organizers and Charts ... 205
- Activity 7-1 Topic-List Graphic Organizer ... 206
- Activity 7-2 Series of Events Graphic Organizer ... 210
- Activity 7-3 Compare-Contrast Graphic Organizer ... 214
- Activity 7-4 Problem-Solution Graphic Organizer ... 218
- Activity 7-5 Question-Answer Graphic Organizer ... 222
- Activity 7-6 Cause-Effect Graphic Organizer ... 226
- Activity 7-7 Series of Steps Chart ... 230
- Activity 7-8 Five W's Chart ... 234
- Activity 7-9 KWL Chart ... 237
- Activity 7-10 What I Have Learned ... 241

Unit 8 — Taking Tests ... 243
- Activity 8-1 The DETER Test Taking Strategy ... 244
- Activity 8-2 Learning About Multiple-Choice Tests ... 245
- Activity 8-3 Doing Well on Multiple-Choice Tests ... 250
- Activity 8-4 Doing Well on True/False Tests ... 255
- Activity 8-5 Demonstrating Mastery of True/False Tests ... 258
- Activity 8-6 Learning About Matching Tests ... 259
- Activity 8-7 Doing Well on Matching Tests ... 261
- Activity 8-8 Learning About Completion Tests ... 263
- Activity 8-9 Guidelines for Taking Completion Tests ... 265
- Activity 8-10 Learning About Essay Tests ... 267
- Activity 8-11 Direction Words in Essay Test Items ... 269
- Activity 8-12 Practice Writing a Response to an Essay Test Item ... 272
- Activity 8-13 Reviewing Your Response to an Essay Test Item ... 273
- Activity 8-14 What I Have Learned ... 274

Contents

Unit 9 — Building Vocabulary Through Word Meaning Clues ... 279
- Activity 9-1 Definition Clues to Word Meaning ... 280
- Activity 9-2 Synonym Clues to Word Meaning ... 282
- Activity 9-3 Antonym Clues to Word Meaning ... 284
- Activity 9-4 Adage Clues to Word Meaning ... 286
- Activity 9-5 Identifying Clues to Word Meaning ... 288
- Activity 9-6 Visual Clues to Word Meaning ... 289
- Activity 9-7 Learning About the Vocabulary Building Strategy ... 293
- Activity 9-8 Using My Vocabulary Words ... 296
- Activity 9-9 Practice Using the Vocabulary Building Strategy: Social Studies ... 300
- Activity 9-10 Practice Using the Vocabulary Building Strategy: Science ... 301
- Activity 9-11 What I Have Learned ... 302

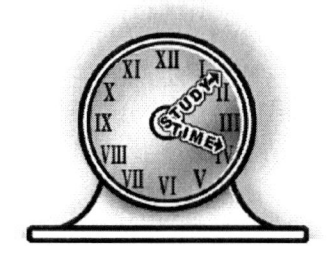

Unit 1
Study Time, Place, Habits, and Goals

Activities

1-1   Managing Study Time

1-2   Monthly Planner

1-3   Practice Preparing a Monthly Planner

1-4   Weekly Planner

1-5   Practice Preparing a Weekly Planner

1-6   Daily Planner

1-7   Practice Preparing a Daily Planner

1-8   My Study Habits

1-9   Improving My Study Habits

1-10   My Study Place

1-11   Improving My Study Place

1-12   Setting Goals

1-13   Practice Setting Goals

1-14   What I Have Learned

Unit 1: Study Time, Place, Habits, and Goals

Activity 1-1: Managing Study Time

Activity 1-1: Managing Study Time

To be successful in school, you must carefully manage your study time. Without careful management of your study time, your studying may be haphazard and ineffective. When managing your study time, consider the continuum of broad (term or semester) to specific (daily). The three components described here will help you to do this.

Monthly Planner: Use a monthly planner for each month of the school term or semester. Prepare blank monthly planners for all months at the beginning of the term or semester. Make entries on your monthly planners as the term or semester progresses. The entries on your monthly planner should be broad, such as "science test."

Weekly Planner: Use a weekly planner for each week of the term or semester. Prepare a weekly planner each Sunday evening. Make additional entries as the week progresses. Your entries should be more detailed on your weekly planner than those on your monthly planner. For example, instead of "science test," you might write "science multiple-choice test on chapters 3-5."

Daily Planner: Use a daily planner for each school day of the term or semester. Prepare a daily planner each evening before a school day. Your entries on a daily planner should be even more detailed than those on your weekly planner. For example, you might write "meet Karen before school to compare our notes for the science test."

Answer the following questions.

1. Why is it important to manage your study time?

2. How would you know how many monthly planners to prepare?

3. When should you prepare a daily planner?

4. Where should you write your least detailed entries?

5. Where should you write your most detailed entries?

Unit 1: Study Time, Place, Habits, and Goals

Activity 1-2: Monthly Planner

Activity 1-2: Monthly Planner

Prepare a blank **monthly planner** for each month of the term or semester at the beginning of the term or semester. Carry all of the monthly planners with you in school. Update them as needed.

Here is what you should enter on a monthly planner.

1. Assignments, tests, and quizzes.

2. In-school activities such as clubs and sports in which you will be involved.

3. Out-of-school activities such as part-time work, recreation, and family events.

Imagine that you are about to prepare a monthly planner for this month or next month. For each category below, write the information you would enter. Keep in mind that your entries should be broad, such as "science test."

Assignments, tests, and quizzes:

_____

_____

_____

_____

In-school activities:

_____

_____

_____

_____

Out-of-school activities:

_____

_____

_____

_____

Unit 1: Study Time, Place, Habits, and Goals

Activity 1-2: Monthly Planner (continued)

Here is an example of a monthly planner prepared by a student named Amanda Warren.

Monthly Planner

Month: September		Year: (this year)		Name: Amanda Warren		
Sunday	**Monday**	**Tuesday**	**Wednesday**	**Thursday**	**Friday**	**Saturday**
			1 School welcome – auditorium	2 Grade Level Mixer	3 Swim team practice	4 Volunteer work at YMCA
5 Visit grandma	6 Labor Day No School	7 Bring gym lock	8 Language club meeting Volunteer work at YMCA	9 Computer assignment due Student Council	10 Prom committee Swim team practice	11
12	13 College prep meeting	14 Math study group Swim team practice	15 Biology lab experiment due	16 Math test Chemistry experiment due	17 Swim meet	18 Volunteer work at YMCA
19 Buy concert tickets	20 History class book report due	21 Swim team practice	22 English quiz Language Club meeting Volunteer work at YMCA	23 Student Council Swim team practice	24 Field trip to science museum	25
26	27	28 English term paper outline due Swim team practice	29 Tryout for drama club	30 Swim team practice Career Fair		

Unit 1: Study Time, Place, Habits, and Goals

Activity 1-3: Practice Preparing a Monthly Planner

Activity 1-3: Practice Preparing a Monthly Planner

Read the following information that a student named Carlos Amaro plans to include in his monthly planner for the month of September. Using the example of Amanda Warren's monthly planner shown in Activity 1-2 as a guide, enter Carlos's information on the blank monthly planner that is provided on the following page.

- Welcome-back reception sponsored by the PTA on the 1st
- Key Club meeting on the 2nd
- Apply for ticket seller job at the Mayfair Cinema on the 17th
- Volunteer work as usher at Biltmore Playhouse each Saturday
- Science study group on the 7th
- Grandparents arrive on the 5th
- Family picnic on the 11th
- Prom Committee on the 22nd
- Intramural softball each Friday
- Work at supermarket Tuesday and Thursday afternoons
- Get local library card on the 3rd
- Topic due for American Literature paper on the 20th
- Tennis w/dad on the 24th
- Brother's birthday party on the 27th
- Planetarium visit on the 13th
- Bring newspaper articles to government class on the 15th
- Vocabulary quiz in Spanish I on the 16th
- Government test on the 20th
- Algebra quiz on the 14th

Unit 1: Study Time, Place, Habits, and Goals

Activity 1-3: Practice Preparing a Monthly Planner (continued)

Monthly Planner

Month:		Year:		Name:		
Sunday	Monday	Tuesday	Wednesday	Thursday	Friday	Saturday
			1	2	3	4
5	6	7	8	9	10	11
12	13	14	15	16	17	18
19	20	21	22	23	24	25
26	27	28	29	30		

Make copies of the blank monthly planner form on the following page so that you have a monthly planner for each month of the term or semester.

Unit 1: Study Time, Place, Habits, and Goals

Activity 1-3: Practice Preparing a Monthly Planner (continued)

Monthly Planner

Month:		Year:		Name:		
Sunday	Monday	Tuesday	Wednesday	Thursday	Friday	Saturday
			1	2	3	4
5	6	7	8	9	10	11
12	13	14	15	16	17	18
19	20	21	22	23	24	25
26	27	28	29	30		

Copyright Mangrum-Strichart Learning Resources
www.mangrum-strichart.com

Unit 1: Study Time, Place, Habits, and Goals

Activity 1-4: Weekly Planner

Activity 1-4: Weekly Planner

A **weekly planner** is an hourly representation of one week within a school term. The entries on a weekly planner should be more detailed than those on a monthly planner, such as "science multiple-choice test on chapters 3-5."

Prepare a weekly planner each Sunday evening before a school week. Carry your weekly planner with you in school. Revise it as needed throughout the week.

Here are the steps to follow when preparing a weekly planner:

1. Enter your classes for each day of the week.

2. Review your monthly planner for the week for which you are preparing the weekly planner. Enter items from the monthly planner for that week. Add more detail.

3. Check your class notes from the week that just ended to determine if there are any additional in-school activities you need to enter.

4. Enter any additional out-of-school activities in which you will be involved.

Imagine that you are about to prepare a weekly planner for this week or next week. For each category below, write the information you would enter on your weekly planner.

Classes:

_____

Items from monthly planner:

_____

Additional in-school activities:

_____

Additional out-of-school activities:

_____

On the following page is an example of a weekly planner for Amanda Warren. Her school day begins at 8:00 and ends at 3:00. You saw an example of her monthly planner for the month of September in Activity 1-2.

Unit 1: Study Time, Place, Habits, and Goals

Activity 1-4: Weekly Planner (continued)

Weekly Planner

Name: Amanda Warren				Week of: 9/19 – 9/25			
Time	Sunday	Monday	Tuesday	Wednesday	Thursday	Friday	Saturday
8:00		Geometry	Geometry	Geometry	Geometry	Geometry	
9:00	Buy concert tickets online	World History (book report due)	World History	World History	World History	Science museum field trip	
10:00		PE	Computer Science	PE	Computer Science	Science museum field trip	Do laundry
11:00		Lunch	Lunch	Lunch	Lunch	Science museum field trip	
12:00		English lit	English lit	English lit (quiz)	English lit	Science museum field trip	Meet Sally at mall
1:00		Biology	Biology	Biology	Biology	Science museum field trip	
2:00		Spanish	Spanish	Spanish	Spanish	Spanish	
After School			3:00 Swim team practice	3:00 Language club meeting	3:00 Student Council Swim team practice		
Evening	Daily Planner Weekly Planner	Daily Planner Homework	Daily Planner Homework	6:00–8:00 Volunteer work YMCA Daily Planner Homework	Daily Planner Homework	8:00 Movies with Sally & Heather	8:00 Pizza date with Brad

Activity 1-5: Practice Preparing a Weekly Planner

Read the following information that Carlos Amaro plans to include in his weekly planner for the week of 9/19 – 9/25. His school day begins at 8:00 and ends at 3:00. You previously worked on Carlos's term planner in Activity 1-3. Using the example of a weekly planner shown in Activity 1-4 as a guide, enter the information below on the blank weekly planner that is provided on the following page.

- Work at supermarket Tuesday and Thursday 4:00 – 6:00
- Government every day at 9:00
- Algebra every day at 11:00
- American Literature paper topic due on Monday
- Band practice on Monday and Wednesday at 1:00
- Chorus on Friday at 1:00
- Art on Tuesday and Thursday at 1:00
- Lunch every day at 12 Noon
- Brother's soccer game Wednesday after school at 4:00
- Bring sheet music to Chorus
- Prom committee meeting Wednesday at 3:00
- Volunteer usher at Biltmore Playhouse on Sat 1:00-4:00
- American Literature every day at 8:00
- PE every day at 2:00
- Intramural softball Friday at 3:00
- Chemistry study group Tuesday after school at 3:00
- Daily Planner Sunday through Thursday
- Algebra study group Thursday after school at 3:00
- Mow lawn Saturday morning
- Study time Sunday afternoon
- Dental appointment Monday at 4:00
- Movie Saturday evening
- Algebra quiz on Thursday
- Government test on Monday
- Tennis with Dad Friday at 7:00
- Chemistry every day at 10:00
- Weekly Planner Sunday
- Homework/Study Time Monday—Thursday evening

Unit 1: Study Time, Place, Habits, and Goals

Activity 1-5: Practice Preparing a Weekly Planner (continued)

Weekly Planner

Name:				Week of:			
Time	Sunday	Monday	Tuesday	Wednesday	Thursday	Friday	Saturday
8:00							
9:00							
10:00							
11:00							
12:00							
1:00							
2:00							
After School							
Evening							

Make copies of the blank weekly planner form on the following page so that you have a weekly planner for each week of the term or semester.

Copyright Mangrum-Strichart Learning Resources
www.mangrum-strichart.com

Unit 1: Study Time, Place, Habits, and Goals

Activity 1-5: Practice Preparing a Weekly Planner (continued)

Weekly Planner

Name:				Week of:			
Time	Sunday	Monday	Tuesday	Wednesday	Thursday	Friday	Saturday

Copyright Mangrum-Strichart Learning Resources
www.mangrum-strichart.com

Unit 1: Study Time, Place, Habits, and Goals

Activity 1-6: Daily Planner

Activity 1-6: Daily Planner

A **daily planner** is a detailed representation of one day within a school week. Prepare a daily planner each evening before a school day. The entries on a daily planner should be even more detailed than those on a weekly planner, such as "meet Karen before school to compare our notes for the science test." Carry your daily planner with you in school each day. Place a √ in front of each item when you accomplish that item.

Here are the steps to follow when preparing a daily planner:

1. Review your weekly planner for the upcoming day. Add the items from your weekly planner to your daily planner for the upcoming day. Provide as much detail as needed for each entry such as specific chapters to read or what to bring to school for a project.

2. Review your daily planner for the day just completed to see if any items you had written there were not accomplished (any item that does not have a √ in front of it). If any of these items must still be accomplished, enter them on the daily planner you are preparing for the upcoming day.

3. Review your class notes for the day just completed to determine if any additional in-school items need to be entered on your daily planner for the upcoming day.

4. Enter any additional out-of-school activities in which you will be involved on the upcoming day.

Imagine that you are about to prepare a daily planner for the upcoming school day. For each category below, write the information you would enter on your daily planner.

Items from weekly planner:

_____

_____

Items from previous daily planner:

_____

_____

Additional in-school activities:

_____

_____

Unit 1: Study Time, Place, Habits, and Goals

Activity 1-6: Daily Planner (continued)

Additional out-of-school activities:
_____
_____

Here is an example of a daily planner for Amanda Warren. Her school day begins at 8:00 and ends at 3:00. You saw examples of her monthly planner for the month of September in Activity 1-2 and her weekly planner for 9/19-9/25 in Activity 1-4.

Daily Planner

Name:	Amanda Warren	Day/Date:	Tuesday 9/21
8:00	Geometry— Go over problems missed on last test. Ask Jim for help with problem 4 from homework		
9:00	World History		
10:00	Computer Science—Bring flash drive		
11:00	Lunch—Remind Sally about going to mall on Saturday		
12:00	English Literature—Purchase novel at book store. Check Internet for reviews and interpretations on Shakespeare's Macbeth		
1:00	Biology—Bring money for field trip		
2:00	Spanish—Bring Don Quixote book		
After School	Swim team practice—3 to 4 Bring new goggles to practice—Bring bathing suit home to wash. Call Maria to go over notes from Biology. Pick up dress from cleaners.		
Evening	Prepare Daily Planner for tomorrow. Do homework. Wash bathing suit. Go on net to look for information for history paper.		

14

Copyright Mangrum-Strichart Learning Resources
www.mangrum-strichart.com

Unit 1: Study Time, Place, Habits, and Goals

Activity 1-7: Practice Preparing a Daily Planner

Activity 1-7: Practice Preparing a Daily Planner

Read the following information that Carlos Amaro plans to include in his daily planner for Thursday, 9/23. His school day begins at 8:00 and ends at 3:00. You previously worked on Carlos's term planner in Activity 1-3 and his weekly planner in Activity 1-6.

Using the example of a daily planner shown in Activity 1-6 as a guide, enter the information below on the blank daily planner provided on the following page.

- Lunch at 12:00—Meet Bob & Gail outside, bring lunch
- Government at 9:00—Bring top hat for role playing a senator
- Evening—Prepare Daily Planner—Do homework and study
- PE at 2:00—Bring catcher's mitt
- Algebra study group at 3:00. Bring last night's homework
- Chemistry at 10:00—Be sure to bring textbook and lab notes
- American Literature at 8:00—Hemingway reading assignment due
- Algebra at 11:00—Quiz—Be on time!
- Evening—Call Janet to talk about chemistry lab
- Art at 1:00—Bring set of pastels
- Work at supermarket 4:00–6:00
- Evening—watch program about Pasteur on Discovery Channel

Unit 1: Study Time, Place, Habits, and Goals

Activity 1-7: Practice Preparing a Daily Planner (continued)

Daily Planner

Name:		Day/Date:
8:00		
9:00		
10:00		
11:00		
12:00		
1:00		
2:00		
After School		
Evening		

Make copies of the blank daily planner form on the following page so that you have a daily planner for each day of the term or semester.

Unit 1: Study Time, Place, Habits, and Goals

Activity 1-7: Practice Preparing a Daily Planner (continued)

Daily Planner

Name:		Day/Date:

Activity 1-8: My Study Habits

Students who get good grades in classes usually have good study habits. They apply their good study habits to all of their classes and school activities.

Read about each of the following good study habits. For each habit, circle Yes if it is something you do most of the time. Circle No if you do not do it most of the time.

I try not to do too much studying at one time. **Yes   No**

- You know you have only so much energy for physical tasks. The same is true for mental tasks like studying. If you try to do too much studying at one time, you will become tired and your studying will not be very effective. Space your study times to be sure you do not try to do too much at once. Taking short breaks as you work on an assignment will help you maintain the mental energy you need to do your studying.

I plan specific times for studying. **Yes   No**

- Study time is any time when you are doing something related to schoolwork. Study time can be doing assigned reading, working on a paper or a project, or studying for a test. It is important to set aside specific times during which you do these things. If you do not, your day may slide by without completing your studying.

I try to study at the same times each day. **Yes   No**

- Studying at the same times each day establishes a routine that can become a regular part of your life, like eating and sleeping. You will come to associate certain times of the day with studying. When these times come, you will be mentally prepared to begin studying.

I set specific goals for my study times. **Yes   No**

- Setting specific goals for your study times will help you to stay focused and monitor your progress. Merely setting aside times for studying is not sufficient. You must be very clear about what you plan to accomplish during your study times.

Unit 1: Study Time, Place, Habits, and Goals

Activity 1-8: My Study Habits (continued)

I start studying when planned. **Yes   No**

- There can be many reasons why you do not start studying at the times you plan. You may delay starting because you do not like an assignment you need to do or you think the assignment is too difficult. Such a delay is called procrastination. Whatever the reason, procrastinating will result in not getting everything done or making careless mistakes as you rush to catch up.

I work on my hardest assignment first. **Yes   No**

- Your hardest assignment will take the most mental energy to complete. It makes sense to do the hardest assignment first since this is when you have the most energy. Save the easier assignments for when your energy may be fading.

I review my notes before beginning an assignment. **Yes   No**

- Many assignments you need to do at home are assignments you start in school. Reviewing your notes from school can help ensure you are doing assignments correctly. Further, your notes may contain important information about an assignment.

I tell my friends not to call me when I am studying. **Yes   No**

- Two study problems can occur if friends call you during your study times. First, your work is interrupted. It is not always easy to get back to studying after an interruption. Also, you may lose the flow of what you were doing. Second, your friends may bring up some things that are not related to your schoolwork that may distract you from what you need to do. Let your friends know other times when they can call you. Turn off your cell phone or do not answer the phone during your study times.

I call another student when I have difficulty with an assignment. **Yes   No**

- Calling another student in your class when you get stuck on an assignment is a good idea. The other student may have an idea that is helpful to you.

Unit 1: Study Time, Place, Habits, and Goals

Activity 1-8: My Study Habits (continued)

I use weekends to review my school work. **Yes** **No**

- Weekends are a great time to have a lot of fun, fulfill household responsibilities, and be involved in family activities. But before very long, another school week is about to begin. You should use part of each weekend to review your schoolwork from the week that ended. This will help you be prepared on Monday morning when another school week begins.

What are some other good study habits. Identify and explain them here.

_____
_____
_____
_____
_____
_____
_____
_____
_____
_____
_____
_____
_____
_____
_____
_____

Activity 1-9: Improving My Study Habits

Look at your answers in Activity 1-8. Each of the study habits described in Activity 1-8 is important for good grades. For each study habit for which you circled No, write that habit next to "Study habit whose use I need to improve." Then write what you will do to improve your use of this study habit.

Study habit whose use I need to improve: _____

What I will do to improve my use of this study habit: _____

_____

Study habit whose use I need to improve: _____

What I will do to improve my use of this study habit: _____

_____

Study habit whose use I need to improve: _____

What I will do to improve my use of this study habit: _____

_____

Study habit whose use I need to improve: _____

What I will do to improve my use of this study habit: _____

_____

Study habit whose use I need to improve: _____

What I will do to improve my use of this study habit: _____

_____

Study habit whose use I need to improve: _____

What I will do to improve my use of this study habit: _____

_____

Study habit whose use I need to improve: _____

What I will do to improve my use of this study habit: _____

_____

Copyright Mangrum-Strichart Learning Resources
www.mangrum-strichart.com

Activity 1-10: My Study Place

Students who get good grades usually have a good study place. They apply their good study habits in this place.

Read about each of the following characteristics of a good study place. For each characteristic, circle Yes if the characteristic is true of your study place. Circle No if it is not true of your study place.

There is nothing to distract me from my studying. **Yes   No**

- Anything in your study place that has nothing to do with studying can distract you from what you must do during your study times. While it may seem that listening to music or a TV broadcast will improve your mood while studying, these things can compete for your attention and may take away from the quality of your work.

There is enough light to see comfortably. **Yes   No**

- The amount of light you need in your study place depends on what you are doing. You might need a certain amount of light when using a computer and a different amount of light when reading a textbook. Be sure you have enough light so that you can clearly see without any strain or discomfort during any study activity.

The temperature can be maintained at a comfortable level. **Yes   No**

- If your study place is too warm, you may become drowsy and even fall asleep. If you are too cold, you may find it hard to think clearly. In either case, your attention to what you are studying will be reduced. Select a temperature that is just right for you.

My study place contains a sufficiently large desk or table. **Yes   No**

- Your study place should include a sufficiently large desk or table that can hold everything you need when you are working on an assignment. Make sure it provides enough space for you to write comfortably.

Unit 1: Study Time, Place, Habits, and Goals

Activity 1-10: My Study Place (continued)

My study place contains an appropriate chair.	**Yes**	**No**

- If the chair in your study place is too comfortable, you may become so relaxed you get drowsy. If the chair is not comfortable, you may not be able to study as long as you planned. Select a chair in which you can sit comfortably yet stay alert for your entire study time period.

My study place contains all the books and materials I need.	**Yes**	**No**

- Be sure to keep in your study place everything you need to do your studying. Your study place should contain writing materials, your textbooks, and reference sources.

My study place contains enough storage space.	**Yes**	**No**

- Your study place should have enough room for all of your class materials and reference sources. Having enough storage space will allow you to keep your desktop or work table free from clutter.

My study place contains a computer if needed.	**Yes**	**No**

- You probably use a computer to do many things involved with your schoolwork. If you do, it is important to have a computer in your study place.

I can use my study place whenever I need to.	**Yes**	**No**

- A study place will do you little good if you cannot use it whenever you need to. If others use your study place for any purpose, you should work out a plan in which times are designated for your use only.

My study place is free from interruptions.	**Yes**	**No**

- Once you start to study, it is important to continue to study without being interrupted. If you need to, hang a sign by your study place that says **DO NOT DISTURB**.

Activity 1-11: Improving My Study Place

Look at your answers in Activity 1-10. Each of the study place characteristics described in Activity 1-10 is important for good grades. For each characteristic for which you circled No, write that characteristic next to "Study place characteristic I need to establish." Then write what you will do to establish this characteristic in your study place.

Study place characteristic I need to establish: _____

What I will do to establish this characteristic: _____

_____

Study place characteristic I need to establish: _____

What I will do to establish this characteristic: _____

_____

Study place characteristic I need to establish: _____

What I will do to establish this characteristic: _____

_____

Study place characteristic I need to establish: _____

What I will do to establish this characteristic: _____

_____

Study place characteristic I need to establish: _____

What I will do to establish this characteristic: _____

_____

Study place characteristic I need to establish: _____

What I will do to establish this characteristic: _____

_____

Study place characteristic I need to establish: _____

What I will do to establish this characteristic: _____

_____

Activity 1-12: Setting Goals

A goal is something you want to achieve. The focus of a goal can be short-term, such as completing a homework assignment or studying for a test you will be having later in the week. The focus of a goal can also be long-term, such as writing a research paper or even getting admitted to a college of your choice.

In Activity 1-8 you learned that setting goals is one of the study habits of successful students. SMARTY is an acronym that will help you remember the six characteristics that you should include in your study goals. Each letter in SMARTY stands for one of the characteristics. Read the information in the box to learn about each.

S Your goals should be **SPECIFIC**. They should clearly indicate what you are going to do.

M Your goals should be **MEASURABLE**. They should allow you to know whether you have achieved your goal.

A Your goals should be **ATTAINABLE**. They should be within your skills and abilities. There is no point in setting goals that you cannot achieve.

R Your goals should be **RELEVANT**. They should be consistent with what you need to do to succeed in school.

T Your goals should have a **TIME FRAME**. They should indicate by when you plan to accomplish your goal.

Y Your goals should be within **YOUR CONTROL**. They should not depend on what others do (unless you are working on a group goal).

Here is an example of a SMARTY goal:

I will locate at least 10 sources of information for my research paper within the next two weeks.

- This goal is *specific* because it tells exactly what must be done.

- This goal is *measurable* because the number of sources located can simply be counted.

- This goal is *attainable* because the number of sources to be located is reasonable.

- This goal is *relevant* because writing a good research paper is related to school success.

Unit 1: Study Time, Place, Habits, and Goals

Activity 1-12: Setting Goals (continued)

- This goal has a *time frame* because it states that it will be accomplished within the next two weeks.
- This goal is within *your control* because its accomplishment doesn't depend on anyone else.

For each letter in SMARTY, write a statement that explains what the letter represents. Underline the most important word in each statement you write.

S _____

_____

M _____

_____

A _____

_____

R _____

_____

T _____

_____

Y _____

_____

Unit 1: Study Time, Place, Habits, and Goals

Activity 1-13: Practice Setting Goals

Activity 1-13: Practice Setting Goals

Write a SMARTY goal for each of the following school subjects. For each goal explain how it meets the characteristics of SMARTY.

1. Science goal: _____

   _____

   _____

   How this goal meets the characteristics of SMARTY.

   _____

   _____

   _____

2. Social Studies goal: _____

   _____

   _____

   How this goal meets the characteristics of SMARTY.

   _____

   _____

   _____

3. Mathematics goal: _____

   _____

   _____

   How this goal meets the characteristics of SMARTY.

   _____

   _____

   _____

Unit 1: Study Time, Place, Habits, and Goals

Activity 1-14: What I Have Learned

Activity 1-14: What I Have Learned

1. What are the three components in the strategy for managing study time?

   _____
   _____
   _____

2. Identify five study habits of successful students.

   _____
   _____
   _____
   _____
   _____

3. Identify five characteristics of a good study place.

   _____
   _____
   _____
   _____
   _____

4. What characteristic does each of the following letters stand for in SMARTY?

   S _____

   M _____

   A _____

   R _____

   T _____

   Y _____

5. Which characteristics of SMARTY are missing in the following goal set by a student?

28

Unit 1: Study Time, Place, Habits, and Goals

Activity 1-14: What I Have Learned (continued)

To impress my teacher, I am going to learn the meanings of tons of new words for my English class tomorrow.

_____

Unit 2
Interpreting and Creating Visual Aids

Activities

2-1   Pictograph

2-2   Create a Pictograph

2-3   Pie Graph

2-4   Create a Pie Graph

2-5   Vertical Bar Graph

2-6   Create a Vertical Bar Graph

2-7   Horizontal Bar Graph

2-8   Create a Horizontal Bar Graph

2-9   Line Graph

2-10 Create a Line Graph

2-11 Table

2-12 Create a Table

2-13 Timeline

2-14 Create a Timeline

2-15 Diagram

2-16 Political Map

2-17 What I Have Learned

Activity 2-1: Pictograph

You will find various types of visual aids in your textbooks and other reading materials. Visual aids are used to show information at a glance. Graphs are one type of visual aid you will find. They are used to represent quantitative information and relationships between entities.

Four types of graphs you will learn about in this unit are a pictograph, pie graph, bar graph, and line graph. In this activity you will learn about a **pictograph**. A pictograph uses pictures or symbols to show information. The title identifies the subject of the pictograph. The legend tells you what each picture or symbol represents.

Look at the horizontal pictograph below. Pictographs are sometimes presented in a vertical format. The pictograph shows the number of cats and dogs adopted at selected animal shelters during the month of April. The legend at the bottom of the pictograph tells you that each symbol stands for 4 animals. Notice that in some cases one half of a symbol is shown, representing 2 animals. The number scale along the bottom axis of the pictograph can also be used to learn how many dogs and cats were adopted at each shelter. Not all pictographs include a number scale.

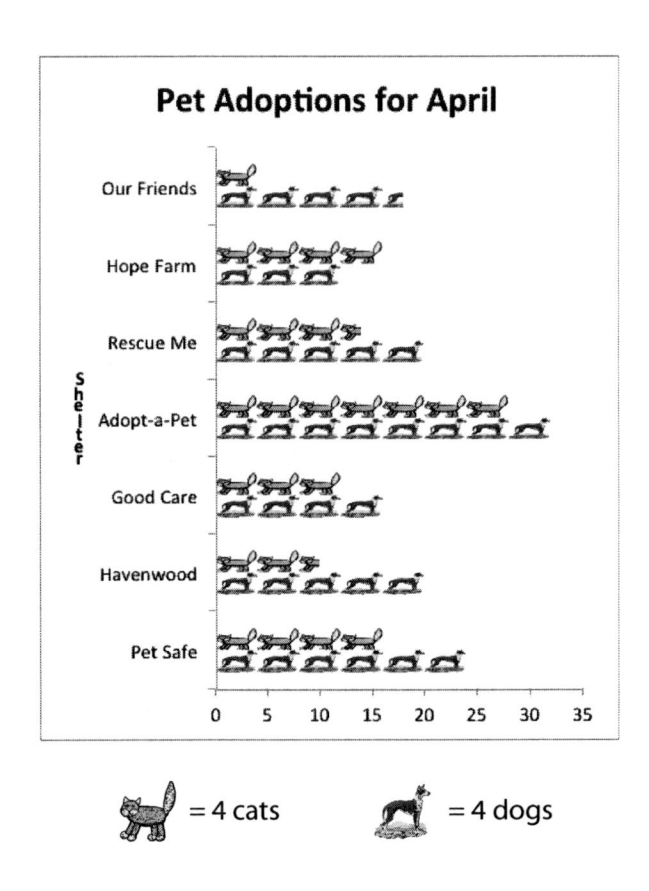

Unit 2: Interpreting and Creating Visual Aids

Activity 2-1: Pictograph (continued)

Use the pictograph shown on the previous page to answer the questions that follow.

1. What does this pictograph show?

   _____

2. What does 🐱 represent? _____

3. Where did you look to learn what 🐕 represents? _____

4. How many shelters are included in this pictograph?

   _____

5. At which shelter were the most dogs adopted? _____

   How many dogs were adopted there? _____

6. At which shelter were the most cats and dogs combined adopted? _____

   How many animals were adopted there? _____

7. At which shelter were the most cats adopted?

   _____

8. How many more dogs than cats were adopted at Good Care?

   _____

9. At which shelter was the number of dogs adopted the same as the number of cats?

   _____

10. At which shelter were more cats adopted than dogs?

    _____

11. Which shelters had the same number of dogs adopted?

    _____

12. How many dog and cats were adopted at all shelters during April?

    _____

Activity 2-2: Create a Pictograph

Here is fictional data that shows the numbers of three types of recreational facilities for selected cities.

City	Parks	Playgrounds	Bike Trails
Greenwood	6	8	12
Thomasville	2	10	4
Hope Valley	12	22	16
Granite	2	8	2
Leisureville	6	2	4
La Vista	10	16	20

Use what you learned in Activity 2-1 to create a pictograph to show this data.

Unit 2: Interpreting and Creating Visual Aids
Activity 2-2: Create a Pictograph (continued)

Now write five questions about the pictograph you just created.

1. _____

2. _____

3. _____

4. _____

5. _____

Write the answer to each of the questions you just wrote.

6. _____

7. _____

8. _____

9. _____

10. _____

Unit 2: Interpreting and Creating Visual Aids

Activity 2-3: Pie Graph

Activity 2-3: Pie Graph

A **pie graph** is a circle divided into segments. It is called a pie graph because it looks like a pie divided into slices. A pie graph is often called a circle graph because of its shape. You will also sometimes see a pie graph referred to as a pie chart.

A pie graph uses percentages to show information. Each segment of a pie graph represents a particular category and shows the percentage of the whole that each category accounts for. Sometimes a segment labeled "Other" combines categories that are too small to show clearly. The segments must add up to 100%.

Look at this pie graph. The title tells you that the graph shows data about active duty U.S. military forces in 2010.

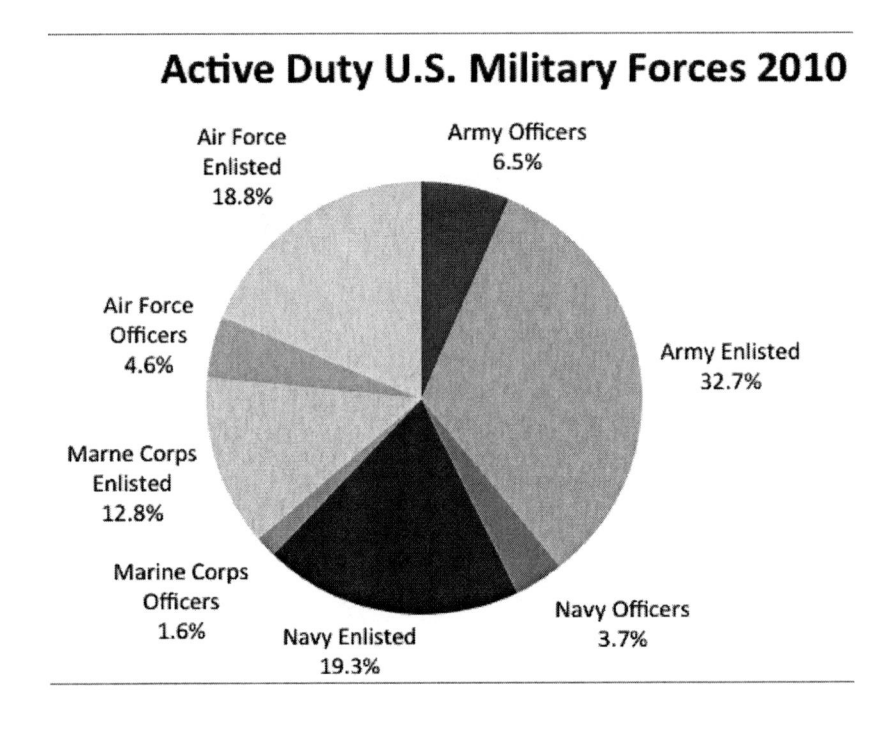

Active Duty U.S. Military Forces 2010

- Air Force Enlisted 18.8%
- Army Officers 6.5%
- Air Force Officers 4.6%
- Army Enlisted 32.7%
- Marne Corps Enlisted 12.8%
- Marine Corps Officers 1.6%
- Navy Enlisted 19.3%
- Navy Officers 3.7%

Unit 2: Interpreting and Creating Visual Aids

Activity 2-3: Pie Graph (continued)

Use the pie graph shown on the previous page to answer the questions that follow.

1. What are two other names for a pie graph?

2. What is this pie graph about?

3. What is the total percentage of all the segments?

4. How many branches of the military are represented in this graph?

5. Which branch had the most officers?

6. Which branch had the least enlisted personnel?

7. Is the percentage of Army officers greater than the percentage of Air Force, Navy, and Marine Corps officers combined?

8. Which branch had the highest ratio of enlisted personnel to officers?

9. The total number of enlisted personnel in 2010 was 1,185,248. How many Air Force enlisted personnel were there? Round your answer to the nearest whole number.

10. How many more Army officers were there than Air Force officers? Round your answer to the nearest whole number.

Activity 2-4: Create a Pie Graph

Here are the sources of U.S. energy production in 2009. The data for each source is the percentage of total U. S. energy produced by that source.

Coal	29.6
Natural gas (dry)	29.5
Crude oil	15.4
Natural plant liquids (NGPL)	3.5
Nuclear electric	11.4
Hydroelectric	3.7
Other	1.6
Biomass	5.3

The data is based on the number of BTUs produced by each energy source (a BTU is the amount of heat needed to raise 1 pound of water 1 degree F). The total number of BTUs produced by all energy sources in 2009 was 72,970 billion.

Use what you learned in Activity 2-3 to create a pie graph that shows this data.

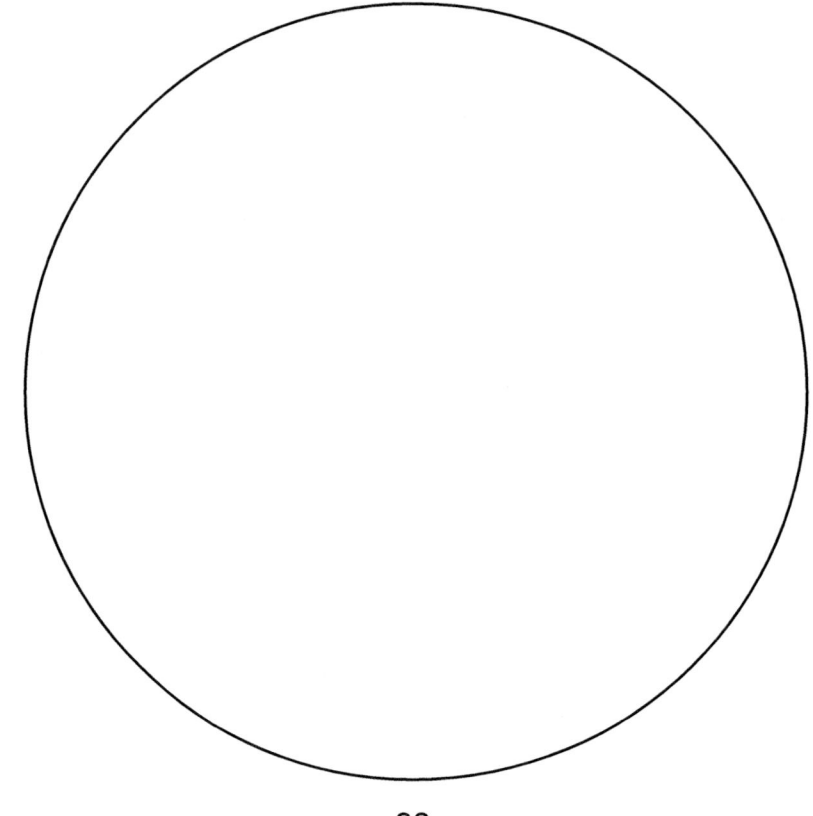

Unit 2: Interpreting and Creating Visual Aids

Activity 2-4: Create a Pie Graph (continued)

Now write five questions about the pie graph you just created.

1. _____

2. _____

3. _____

4. _____

5. _____

Write the answer to each of the questions you just wrote.

6. _____

7. _____

8. _____

9. _____

10. _____

Activity 2-5: Vertical Bar Graph

A bar graph is a graphical display that represents data in different categories or groups. A bar graph may be vertical or horizontal. The bar graph shown in this activity is a **vertical bar graph**. You will see a horizontal bar graph in Activity 2-7.

On a vertical bar graph, a number line goes up the left axis of the graph. The label on the left axis of the graph tells what the numbers represent. The labels along the bottom axis of the graph tell what each bar represents. The higher the bar, the greater the value of whatever the bar represents. Often, the numerical value for a bar is shown. This is done so that you do not have to estimate the height of each bar. If there are bars of more than one color or shading, a legend is provided to identify what each color or shade represents.

Look at this vertical bar graph. It shows highway and city miles per gallon (MPG) for the cars that got the best gas mileage in 2009. The higher the bar, the better the gas mileage. The legend has been placed at the right side of the graph. Using this graph, you can compare the highway and city gas mileage for the eight cars.

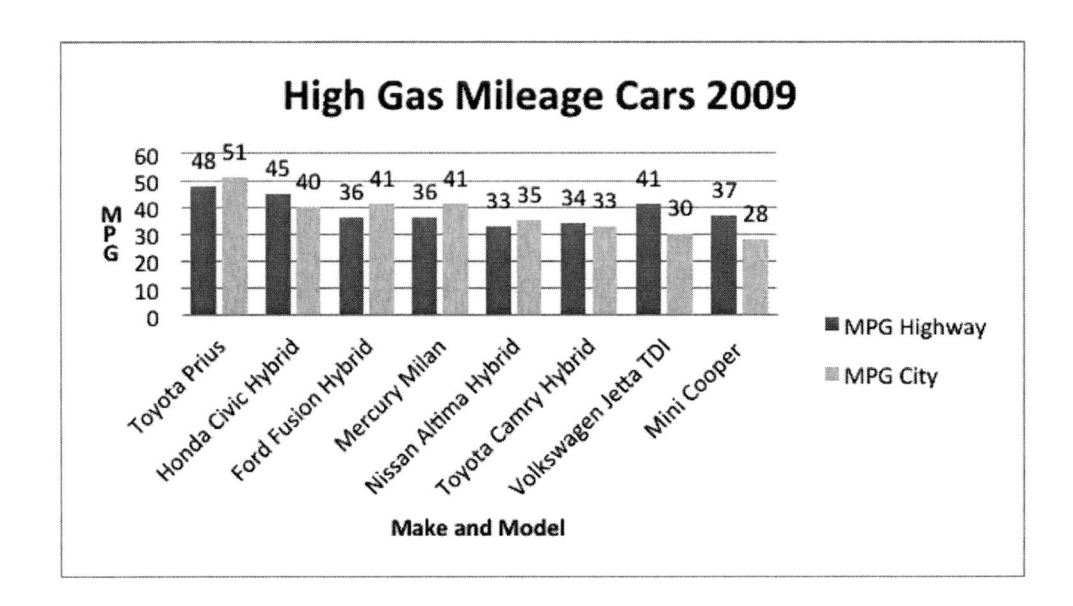

High Gas Mileage Cars 2009

Make and Model	MPG Highway	MPG City
Toyota Prius	48	51
Honda Civic Hybrid	45	40
Ford Fusion Hybrid	36	41
Mercury Milan	36	41
Nissan Altima Hybrid	33	35
Toyota Camry Hybrid	34	33
Volkswagen Jetta TDI	41	30
Mini Cooper	37	28

Unit 2: Interpreting and Creating Visual Aids

Activity 2-5: Vertical Bar Graph (continued)

Use the vertical bar graph shown on the previous page to answer the questions that follow.

1. What is this graph about?

2. Which car had the highest city gas mileage?

3. If you were to do a lot of city driving, which car would be your poorest choice to save money on gas?

4. Which two cars had the same highway gas mileage?

5. Which cars had higher city gas mileage than highway gas mileage?

6. If exactly half of your driving is in the city, and half on the highway, how many miles per gallon could you expect to get from the Ford Fusion Hybrid?

7. Which car had the greatest difference between its highway and city gas mileage?

8. Which car had the smallest difference between its highway and city gas mileage?

9. You drove your Mercury Milan Hybrid on the highway. You used three and one half gallons of gas. How many miles did you drive on the highway?

10. Gas cost $3 a gallon. Last week, you drove your Volkswagen Jetta TDI 120 miles in the city. How much money would you have saved if you had driven a Honda Civic Hybrid instead?

Activity 2-6: Create a Vertical Bar Graph

Population density is the number of persons living in an area per square mile. Here is population density data for eight states for three years.

State	1990	2000	2010
Utah	21	27	34
New Jersey	1051	1144	1196
Florida	241	298	351
Michigan	164	176	175
Texas	65	80	96
Illinois	206	224	231
Iowa	50	52	55
Georgia	113	142	168

Use what you learned in Activity 2-5 to create a vertical bar graph that shows this data.

Unit 2: Interpreting and Creating Visual Aids

Activity 2-6: Create a Vertical Bar Graph (continued)

Now write five questions about the vertical bar graph you just created.

1. _____

2. _____

3. _____

4. _____

5. _____

Write the answer to each of the questions you just wrote.

6. _____

7. _____

8. _____

9. _____

10. _____

Activity 2-7: Horizontal Bar Graph

On a **horizontal bar graph**, the labels on the left axis tell what each bar represents. The label at the bottom axis of the graph tells what the numbers represent. The longer the bar, the greater the numerical value of whatever the bar represents.

Look at this horizontal bar graph. It shows the annual income and expenditures for eight countries converted to U.S. dollars. A legend is provided to show what each shaded bar represents.

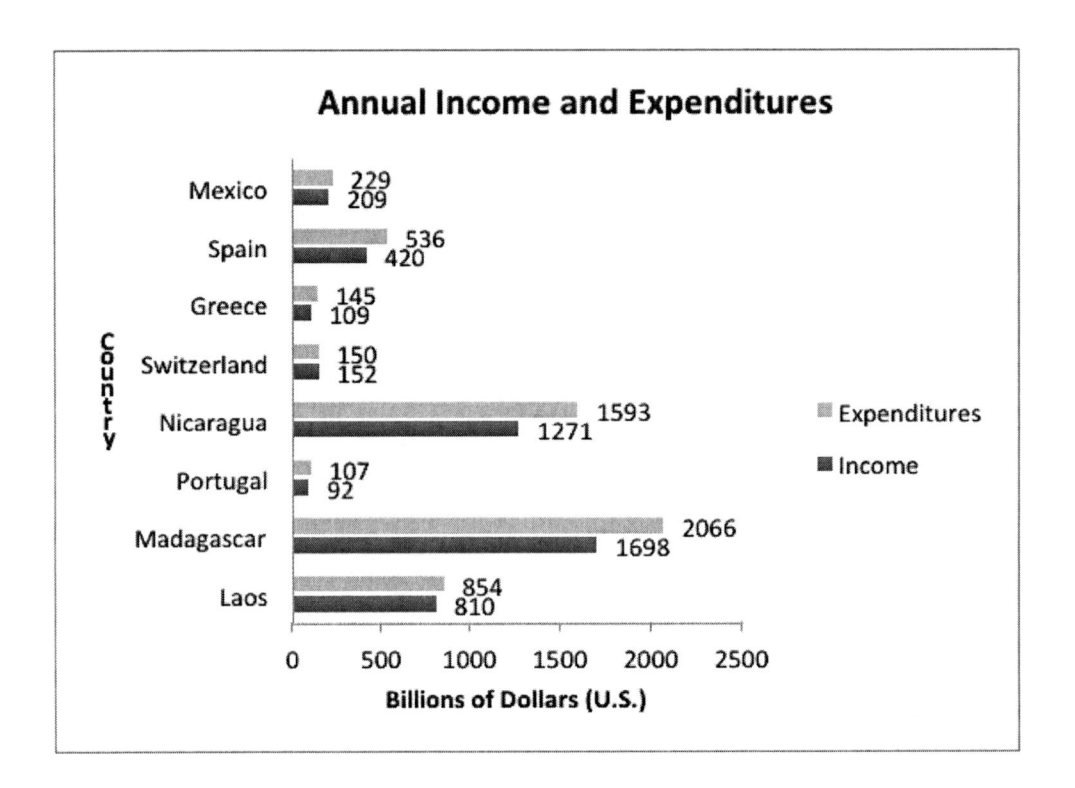

Annual Income and Expenditures

Country	Expenditures	Income
Mexico	229	209
Spain	536	420
Greece	145	109
Switzerland	150	152
Nicaragua	1593	1271
Portugal	107	92
Madagascar	2066	1698
Laos	854	810

Billions of Dollars (U.S.)

Unit 2: Interpreting and Creating Visual Aids

Activity 2-7: Horizontal Bar Graph (continued)

Use the horizontal bar graph shown on the previous page to answer the questions that follow.

1. What is this bar graph about?

2. Which country had the lowest income?

3. Which country had the highest expenditures?

4. Which country had the highest income?

5. How much more income would Spain need in order to equal its expenditures?

6. Did the country with the highest expenditures also have the highest income?

7. Which country other than Madagascar had the largest difference between its expenditures and its income?

8. Which country had higher income than expenditures?

9. How much greater was Greece's expenditures than its income?

10. What conclusion can you reach by studying this graph?

Activity 2-8: Create a Horizontal Bar Graph

Here are the number of gold, silver, and bronze medals won by eight countries at the 2008 Summer Olympics, held in Beijing, China.

Country	Gold	Silver	Bronze
Hungary	3	5	2
Brazil	3	4	8
United States	36	38	36
Japan	9	6	10
China	51	21	28
Australia	14	15	17
Jamaica	6	3	2
France	7	16	17

Use what you learned in Activity 2-7 to create a horizontal bar graph that shows this data.

Unit 2: Interpreting and Creating Visual Aids

Activity 2-8: Create a Horizontal Bar Graph (continued)

Now write five questions about the horizontal bar graph you just created.

1. _____

2. _____

3. _____

4. _____

5. _____

Write the answer to each of the questions you just wrote.

6. _____

7. _____

8. _____

9. _____

10. _____

Activity 2-9: Line Graph

A **line graph** is generally used to show information over a period of time. It is useful for comparing things at different times and seeing trends or patterns. A number line goes up the left axis of the graph. The label for the left axis of the graph tells what the numbers represent. The period of time represented by the graph is shown along the bottom axis. Symbols are used to show how much there is of what the numbers represent. The higher the symbol is placed on the graph, the greater the value of whatever the symbol represents. The symbols are connected by lines. The legend shows what each symbol represents.

Look at this line graph. It shows unemployment rates for three countries from 1960 to 2010. Unemployment rate is expressed as the percentage of the work force that is unemployed at any given date.

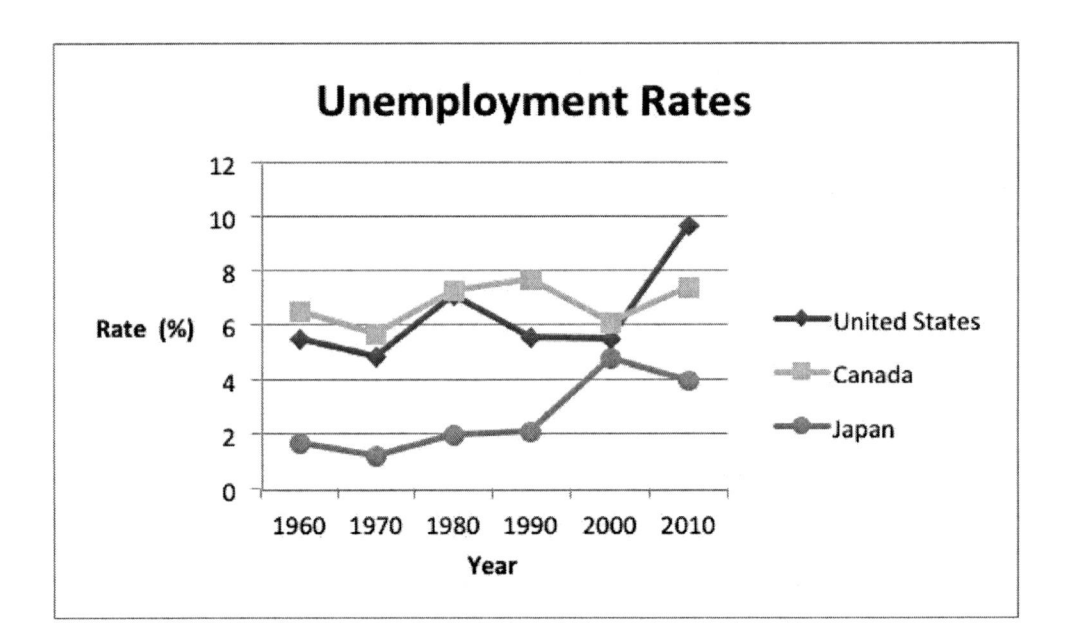

Unit 2: Interpreting and Creating Visual Aids

Activity 2-9: Line Graph (continued)

Use the line graph shown on the previous page to answer the following questions.

1. What is this line graph about?

2. Which country is represented by a circle?

3. How many years are there between each data point?

4. Which year showed the greatest increase in unemployment for the United States?

5. In what year did the unemployment rate for the United States surpass that of Canada?

6. How would you describe Japan's unemployment rate from 1960 to 1990?

7. In what year were the unemployment rates for the three countries fairly similar?

8. The unemployment rate is an indicator of the health of the economy. Which country has maintained the healthiest economy over the years shown?

9. Is there a clear trend for unemployment in the United States for the years shown?

10. What information would you need to determine the number of people in the work force who were unemployed in the United States in 2000?

Activity 2-10: Create a Line Graph

Here are the 24-hour average temperatures for three major world cities. The temperatures are shown using the Fahrenheit scale.

City	Jan	March	May	July	Sept	Nov
London, England	43	46	56	66	61	48
Beijing, China	24	41	68	79	68	39
Rome, Italy	45	51	64	76	70	53

Use what you learned in Activity 2-9 to create a line graph that shows this data.

Unit 2: Interpreting and Creating Visual Aids

Activity 2-10: Create a Line Graph (continued)

Now write five questions about the line graph you just created.

1. _____

2. _____

3. _____

4. _____

5. _____

Write the answer to each of the questions you just wrote.

6. _____

7. _____

8. _____

9. _____

10. _____

Unit 2: Interpreting and Creating Visual Aids

Activity 2-11: Table

Activity 2-11: Table

A **table** is an efficient way to show a lot of information in one place. The title tells you what the table is about. The heading at the top of each column tells what information you will find in that column.

Look at this table. It presents information about the countries that constitute Central America.

\multicolumn{6}{c}{Countries of Central America}
Country	Area in Square Miles	Coastline in Miles	Population	Capital	Monetary Unit
Belize	8,867	240	314,522	Belmopan	Belizean dollar
Costa Rica	19,730	801	4,516,220	San José	Costa Rica colón
El Salvador	8,124	191	6,052,064	San Salvador	U.S. dollar
Guatemala	42,042	248	13,276,517	Guatemala City	quetzal
Honduras	43,278	509	7,792,854	Tegucigalpa	lempira
Nicaragua	49,998	565	5,891,199	Managua	córdova
Panama	30,193	546	3,360,474	Panama City	balboa

Unit 2: Interpreting and Creating Visual Aids

Activity 2-11: Table (continued)

Use the table shown on the previous page to answer the questions that follow.

1. How many countries are there in Central America?

2. What five things can you learn about each country?

3. Which country has the largest area?

4. Which country has the smallest population?

5. Which country has the longest coastline?

6. What is the monetary unit of Guatemala?

7. How many more people live in Honduras than in Panama?

8. How much larger in area is Honduras than Costa Rica?

9. What is the capital of Belize?

10. What is the total population of Central America?

11. In which country would an American traveler not have to worry about making a currency exchange?

12. Which countries do not border a body of water?

53

Activity 2-12: Create a Table

Read the following information about the New England states.

Connecticut is nicknamed the Nutmeg State. Its population is 3,518,288, who reside in an area of 5,543 square miles. The capital is Hartford. Connecticut's state flower is the Mountain Laurel, while its state bird is the American Robin.

Rhode Island, often called the Ocean State, has a population of 1,053,219. Not surprisingly, its state bird is the Rhode Island Red. The area of Rhode Island is only 1,545 square miles. It is the smallest state in the U.S. Providence is the capital city. Rhode Island decided to name the Violet as its state flower.

Maine's capital is Augusta, while its nickname is the Pine Tree State. Maine has a population of 1,318,301 people spread within 33,385 square miles. The Chickadee is the state bird and the White Pinecone its designated flower.

The population of Massachusetts is 6,593,587, while its area is 10,555 square miles. Fittingly, the state flower of Massachusetts is the Mayflower. Its state bird is the same as Maine's. Boston, the home of the Red Sox, is its capital city. Massachusetts is sometimes called the Bay State.

If you are in Montpelier, you are in the capital city of Vermont. Often referred to as the Green Mountain State, Vermont has a population of only 621,760. Its area is 9,614 square miles. The Red Clover is Vermont's state flower, while the Hermit Thrush is its state bird.

If you were ever asked which state is nicknamed the Granite State, reply New Hampshire. A total of 1,324,575 people live within its area of 9,350 square miles. If you are booking a trip to its capital, make sure you get a ticket to Concord. Check out the beautiful flowers, especially its state flower, the Purple Lilac. Purple must be a popular color in New Hampshire since its state bird is the Purple Finch.

Use what you learned in Activity 2-11 to create a table that shows this information.

Unit 2: Interpreting and Creating Visual Aids

Activity 2-12: Create a Table (continued)

Unit 2: Interpreting and Creating Visual Aids

Activity 2-12: Create a Table (continued)

Now write five questions about the table you just created.

1. _____

2. _____

3. _____

4. _____

5. _____

Write the answer to each of the questions you just wrote.

6. _____

7. _____

8. _____

9. _____

10. _____

Activity 2-13: Timeline

A **timeline** shows in chronological order when important events of a certain nature occurred. The events may be shown in either a horizontal or a vertical format.

Look at this vertical timeline. It shows the dates when the United States became involved in armed conflicts during the 20th century. The events are shown in chronological order from the earliest event at the top to the most recent event at the bottom. Notice that minimal detail is provided for each entry.

U.S. Conflicts During the 20th Century

1917	U.S. joins allies in World War I.
1941	Pearl Harbor attacked. U.S. enters World War II.
1950	U.S. leads fifteen other nations in the Korean War.
1964	U.S. becomes involved in the Vietnam War.
1983	U.S. invades Grenada to establish order and eliminate Cuban military presence.
1989	U.S. sends troops to Panama to capture Manuel Noriega, who had been indicted for drug trafficking.
1991	U.S. leads coalition of 32 countries in Persian Gulf War to drive Iraq out of Kuwait.
1994	U.S. invades Haiti to restore president Jean-Betrand Aristide to power.
1999	U.S. leads NATO forces in use of air strikes to protect Yugoslavia's province of Kosovo from Serbian attacks.

Unit 2: Interpreting and Creating Visual Aids

Activity 2-13: Timeline (continued)

Use the timeline shown on the previous page to answer the questions that follow.

1. What does this timeline show?

2. How many years elapsed between the U.S.'s entry in World War I and its entry in World War II?

3. How many countries were in the coalition to drive Iraq from Kuwait?

4. Which came earlier – the U.S.'s armed involvement in Haiti or in Panama?

5. What event caused the U.S. to enter World War II?

6. How many years after becoming involved in the Korean War did the U.S. become involved in the Vietnam War?

7. Which Yugoslovian province was protected by NATO air strikes?

8. How many armed conflicts was the U.S. involved in during the 20th century?

9. Which armed conflict was brought about by criminal activity?

10. How many years did the Korean War last?

Activity 2-14: Create a Timeline

Here is information about buildings that figured prominently in the history of tall buildings.

Building	Location	Date Built	Height (ft)	Floors
Sears Tower	Chicago	1974	1,450	110
Taipei 101	Taiwan	2004	1,670	101
Woolworth Building	New York City	1913	792	60
Petronas Towers	Malaysia	1998	1,483	88
Manhattan Life	New York City	1894	348	18
Empire State Building	New York City	1931	1,250	102
Burj Khalifa	United Arab Emerites	2010	2,716	160
Chrysler Building	New York City	1930	1,046	77

Use what you learned in Activity 2-13 to create a horizontal timeline that shows this information.

Unit 2: Interpreting and Creating Visual Aids

Activity 2-14: Create a Timeline (continued)

Now write five questions about the timeline you just created.

1. _____

2. _____

3. _____

4. _____

5. _____

Write the answer to each of the questions you just wrote.

6. _____

7. _____

8. _____

9. _____

10. _____

Unit 2: Interpreting and Creating Visual Aids

Activity 2-15: Diagram

Activity 2-15: Diagram

A **diagram** is a drawing that shows the parts of an object or thing and the relationships between the parts. The parts are labeled.

Look at this diagram that shows the major parts of a space shuttle. For this activity, the parts are not labeled. There are lines on which you can write the name of each part to which an arrow points. Read the information on the following page that describes each of the parts of a space shuttle. Use the information to label each part of the diagram.

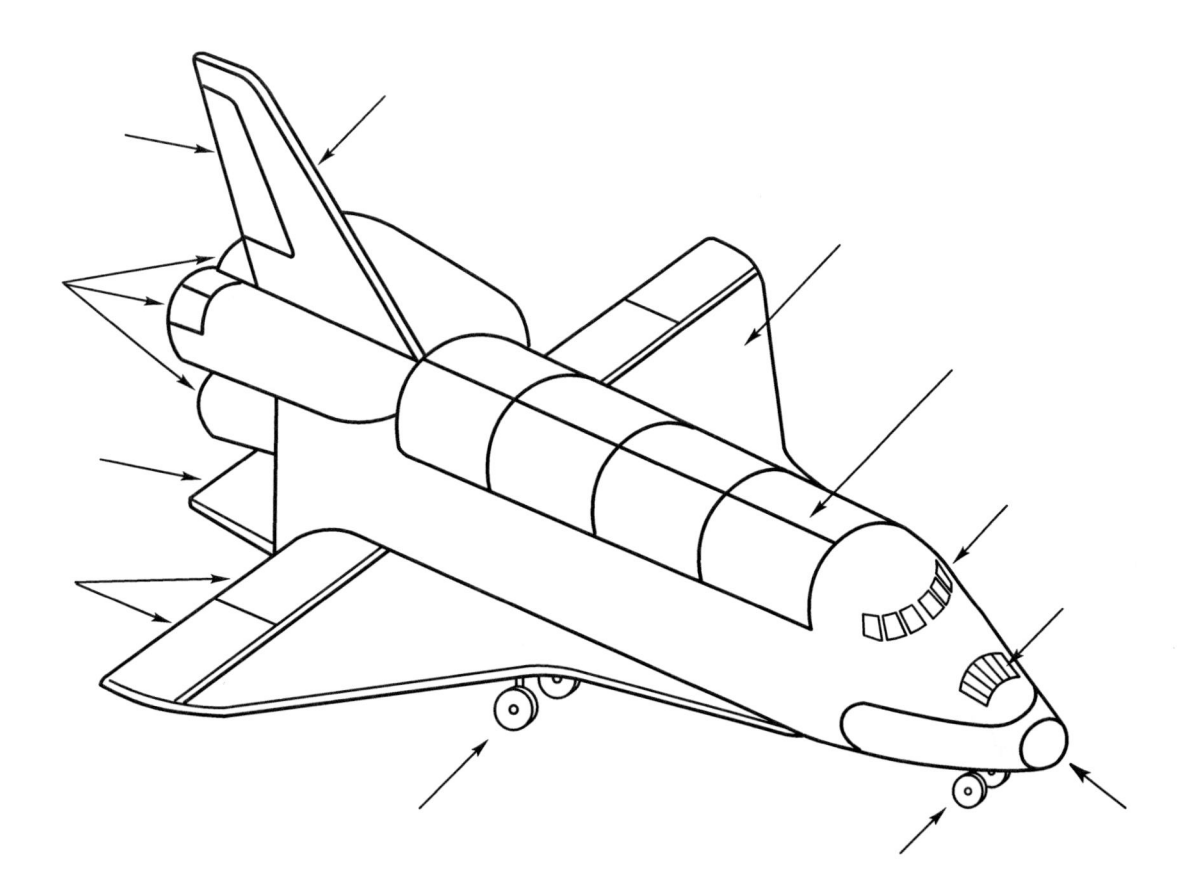

61

Body Flap—a flap located at the bottom rear of the shuttle. It is used during descent to control the motion of pitch.

Delta Wings—the triangular-shaped wings on each side of the space shuttle.

Elevons—flaps located on the trailing edge of each wing. They are used to control pitch and roll once a returning space shuttle enters the atmosphere.

Engines—located at the rear of the space shuttle. These include the main propulsion engines and the orbital maneuvering system engines.

Flight Deck—the part in the front of the space shuttle where the crew sits for launch and landing.

Forward Control Thrusters—small engines located on the nose of the space shuttle. They are used to maneuver the shuttle in space.

Main Landing Gear—the wheels used for landing located at the rear of the space shuttle.

Nose Cone—the front of the space shuttle.

Nose Landing Gear—the wheels used for landing located at the front of the space shuttle.

Payload Doors—the curved doors located on the top of the space shuttle that open to the cargo bay inside the space shuttle.

Split Rudder/Speed Brake—a divided flap located along the back edge of the vertical tail. The rudder part controls the movement of the nose of the shuttle to the left and right, while the brake part increases drag and slows the space shuttle during descent and landing.

Tail Section—the fin at the top back of the space shuttle that provides stability while the space shuttle is flying.

Unit 2: Interpreting and Creating Visual Aids

Activity 2-16: Political Map

Activity 2-16: Political Map

The type of map you will most often use in school is a **political map**. A political map shows governmental boundaries. Depending on the map, a political map might show boundaries of countries, states, provinces, and/or counties. The location of major cities is usually included.

Look at this political map of Argentina.

Source: Used with permission of MAPS.com

The map shows the major cities in Argentina. The dot next to the name of each city shows its location. A large dot by the name of a city indicates that city has a large population. The dot that is circled identifies the capital city of Argentina. The map also shows the countries that border Argentina as well as the location of the Pacific and Atlantic oceans.

There is a map scale that allows you to measure distances between cities in either miles or kilometers. The map also shows latitude and longitude. The compass rose at the top left of the map shows direction.

Unit 2: Interpreting and Creating Visual Aids

Activity 2-16: Political Map (continued)

Use the political map of Argentina shown on the previous page to answer the following questions.

1. What does this map show?

2. What is the capital of Argentina?

3. What countries border Argentina?

4. What is one of the cities in Argentina that has a large population?

5. Which of the cities shown in Argentina is furthest south?

6. What is the capital of Uruguay?

7. What islands are found off the southeast coast of Argentina?

8. Which city is further west – Salta or Mendoza?

9. What is the approximate latitude of the capital of Argentina?

10. What is the approximate longitude of Rawson?

11. Approximately how many miles is the distance between Cordova and Santa Rosa?

12. Is the distance from Gadoy Cruz to Rosario less than 500 kilometers?

Activity 2-17: What I Have Learned

Answer the following questions.

1. What should you use to show the dates of important events over a period of time?

2. What are two other names for a pie graph?

3. What allows you to measure distances between points on a map?

4. What should you use to show a great deal of information in a condensed space?

5. What does a political map show?

6. Which type of graph is best for showing information over a period of time?

7. Which type of graph uses pictures or drawings to display information?

8. Which is a longer distance – 85 miles or 85 kilometers?

9. Where is the most recent event shown on a vertical timeline?

10. Can a vertical bar graph and a horizontal bar graph be used interchangeably?

Unit 3
Reading and Taking Notes from Textbooks

Activities

3-1   Learning About the PQRW Strategy

3-2   The Preview Step

3-3   The Question, Read, and Write Steps

3-4   Practice Using PQRW

3-5   Practice Using PQRW

3-6   Practice Using PQRW

3-7   What I Have Learned

Activity 3-1: Learning About the PQRW Strategy

The best way to understand the information in your textbooks is to be an active reader. The best way to be an active reader is to take written notes. When writing notes, you have to actively engage the information. Your notes will be a valuable tool when you study for tests.

Textbooks vary in how their chapters are organized. In most cases, chapters are divided into parts. The parts may be called sections, lessons, or units. Sometimes the parts are identified numerically as in 12.1, 12.2, and so on. In this example, 12.1 refers to the first part of chapter 12.

The major component of a textbook chapter is the information the chapter provides about a subject. You will also find additional features that are designed to help you fully understand the information. Examples of such features include objectives, key ideas, key terms, important people, significant places, anecdotal stories, reading checks, skills applications, writing activities, definitions, guiding questions, checkpoints, and assessments. Many textbook chapters also direct you to the Internet for further learning. These features are supplemental to the basic information provided in the chapter. They are there for you to use as needed. Your teacher may or may not require you to use them.

PQRW is a four-step strategy for reading textbook chapters and taking written notes from chapters in textbooks. The strategy can be used if you are required to read the entire chapter as an assignment, or if you are assigned to read the chapter part by part.

The four steps in the strategy are:

P = Preview

Q = Question

R = Read

W = Write

Answer the following questions.

1. What are three names that may be given to the parts into which a chapter is divided?

   _____

   _____

   _____

Unit 3: Reading and Taking Notes from Textbooks

Activity 3-1: Learning About the PQRW Strategy (continued)

2. You are beginning to read a part of a textbook chapter that is identified as 11.3. What does 11.3 tell you?

   _____

3. Are all textbook chapters divided into parts?

   _____

4. What is the major component of a textbook chapter?

   _____

5. What are five features you may find in a textbook chapter that are designed to help you fully understand the information that is presented?

   _____

   _____

   _____

   _____

   _____

6. Next to each letter, write the step that the letter stands for in the PQRW strategy.

   P _____

   Q _____

   R _____

   W _____

Activity 3-2: The Preview Step

The purpose of the **preview** step is to help you quickly obtain an idea of what a chapter or chapter part is about. Here is what to do in the preview step.

- Read the *title* at the beginning of the chapter or chapter part. The title will give you a very general sense of what the chapter or chapter part is about.

- Read the *introduction* to the chapter or chapter part. This is the first section of text after the title and is typically brief. An introduction alerts you to the information that will follow. Sometimes an introduction is not provided.

- Read all of the *headings* in the chapter or chapter part. Doing this will give you a good idea of the specific information that is covered in the chapter or chapter part.

- Look at any *visual aids* such as illustrations, tables, graphs, and diagrams in the chapter or chapter part. Read their titles and captions. This will add to your idea of what the chapter or chapter part is about.

- Read the *summary* or *conclusion* at the end of the chapter or chapter part. A summary restates the main points. A conclusion provides a generalization derived from the facts and ideas presented. Some textbook chapters or chapter parts do not provide either a summary or a conclusion.

On the pages that follow is Section 1 of a chapter part of a high school textbook titled "World History." The title of the chapter is "Life in The Industrial Age 1800-1914." The chapter is divided into four sections.

Complete the preview step for Section 1. Then answer the questions that follow Section 1.

The Industrial Revolution Spreads

WITNESS HISTORY 🔊 AUDIO

The Steelmaking Process
By the 1880s, steel had replaced steam as the great symbol of the Industrial Revolution. In huge steel mills, visitors watched with awe as tons of molten metal were poured into giant mixers:

❝ At night the scene is indescribably wild and beautiful. The flashing fireworks, the terrific gusts of heat, the gaping, glowing mouth of the giant chest, the quivering light from the liquid iron, the roar of a near-by converter . . . combine to produce an effect on the mind that no words can translate. ❞
—J. H. Bridge, *The Inside History of the Carnegie Steel Company*

Focus Question How did science, technology, and big business promote industrial growth?

Painting of a nineteenth-century steel mill

Objectives
- List the industrial powers that emerged in the 1800s.
- Describe the impact of new technology on industry, transportation, and communication.
- Understand how big business emerged in the late 1800s.

Terms, People, and Places

Henry Bessemer	assembly line
Alfred Nobel	Orville and Wilbur Wright
Michael Faraday	Guglielmo Marconi
dynamo	stock
Thomas Edison	corporation
interchangeable parts	cartel

Note Taking

Reading Skill: Identify Main Ideas Fill in a chart like this one with the major developments of the Industrial Revolution.

The Second Industrial Revolution		
New Powers	Industry/Business	Transportation/Communication
•	•	•
•	•	•

298 Life in the Industrial Age

The first phase of industrialization had largely been forged from iron, powered by steam engines, and driven by the British textile industry. By the mid-1800s, the Industrial Revolution entered a second phase. New industrial powers emerged. Factories powered by electricity used innovative processes to turn out new products. Changes in business organization contributed to the rise of giant companies. As the twentieth century dawned, this second Industrial Revolution transformed the economies of the Western world.

New Industrial Powers Emerge

During the early Industrial Revolution, Britain stood alone as the world's industrial giant. To protect its head start, Britain tried to enforce strict rules against exporting inventions.

For a while, the rules worked. Then, in 1807, British mechanic William Cockerill opened factories in Belgium to manufacture spinning and weaving machines. Belgium became the first European nation after Britain to industrialize. By the mid-1800s, other nations had joined the race, and several newcomers were challenging Britain's industrial supremacy.

Nations Race to Industrialize How were other nations able to catch up with Britain so quickly? First, nations such as Germany, France, and the United States had more abundant supplies of coal, iron, and other resources than did Britain. Also, they had the advantage of being able to follow Britain's lead. Like Belgium, latecomers often borrowed British experts or technology. The first American textile factory was built in Pawtucket, Rhode Island, with plans smuggled out of Britain. American inventor Robert Fulton powered his steamboat with one of James Watt's steam engines.

Two countries in particular—Germany and the United States—thrust their way to industrial leadership. Germany united into a powerful nation in 1871. Within a few decades, it became Europe's leading industrial power. Across the Atlantic, the United States advanced even more rapidly, especially after the Civil War. By 1900, the United States was manufacturing about 30 percent of the world's industrial goods, surpassing Britain as the leading industrial nation.

Uneven Development Other nations industrialized more slowly, particularly those in eastern and southern Europe. These nations often lacked natural resources or the capital to invest in industry. Although Russia did have resources, social and political conditions slowed its economic development. Only in the late 1800s, more than 100 years after Britain, did Russia lumber toward industrialization.

In East Asia, however, Japan offered a remarkable success story. Although Japan lacked many basic resources, it industrialized rapidly after 1868 because of a political revolution that made modernization a priority. Canada, Australia, and New Zealand also built thriving industries during this time.

Effects of Industrialization Like Britain, the new industrial nations underwent social changes, such as rapid urbanization. Men, women, and children worked long hours in difficult and dangerous conditions. As you will read, by 1900, these conditions had begun to improve in many industrialized nations.

The factory system produced huge quantities of new goods at lower prices than ever before. In time, ordinary workers were buying goods that in earlier days only the wealthy could afford. The demand for goods created jobs, as did the building of cities, railroads, and factories. Politics changed, too, as leaders had to meet the demands of an industrial society.

Globally, industrial nations competed fiercely, altering patterns of world trade. Because of their technological and economic advantage, the Western powers came to <u>dominate</u> the world more than ever before.

Checkpoint What factors led to the industrialization of other nations after Britain?

Technology Sparks Industrial Growth

During the early Industrial Revolution, inventions such as the steam engine were generally the work of gifted tinkerers. They experimented with simple machines to make them better. By the 1880s, the pace of change quickened as companies hired professional chemists and engineers to create new products and machinery. The union of science, technology, and industry spurred economic growth.

Steel Production and the Bessemer Process American inventor William Kelly and British engineer Henry Bessemer independently developed a new process for making steel from iron. In 1856, Bessemer

---

Vocabulary Builder
<u>dominate</u>—(DAHM uh nayt) *v.* to rule or control by power or influence

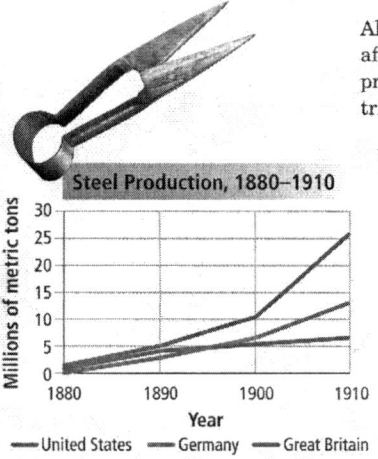

Steel Production, 1880–1910

— United States — Germany — Great Britain

Graph Skills By the late 1800s, steel was the major material used in manufacturing tools, such as the sheep shears (above). The graph shows the amount of steel produced by the United States, Germany, and Great Britain. Between 1890 and 1910, which nation had the greatest increase in steel production? The smallest?

SOURCES: *European Historical Statistics, 1750–1970; Historical Statistics of the United States*

300 Life in the Industrial Age

patented this process. Steel was lighter, harder, and more durable than iron, so it could be produced very cheaply. Steel quickly became the major material used in tools, bridges, and railroads.

As steel production soared, industrialized countries measured their success in steel output. In 1880, for example, the average German steel mill produced less than 5 million metric tons of steel a year. By 1910, that figure reached nearly 15 million metric tons.

Innovations in Chemistry Chemists created hundreds of new products, from medicines such as aspirin to perfumes and soaps. Newly developed chemical fertilizers played a key role in increasing food production.

In 1866, the Swedish chemist Alfred Nobel invented dynamite, an explosive much safer than others used at the time. It was widely used in construction and, to Nobel's dismay, in warfare. Dynamite earned Nobel a huge fortune, which he willed to fund the famous Nobel prizes that are still awarded today.

Electric Power Replaces Steam In the late 1800s, a new power source—electricity—replaced steam as the dominant source of industrial power. Scientists like Benjamin Franklin had tinkered with electricity a century earlier. The Italian scientist Alessandro Volta developed the first battery around 1800. Later, the English chemist Michael Faraday created the first simple electric motor and the first dynamo, a machine that generates electricity. Today, all electrical generators and transformers work on the principle of Faraday's dynamo.

In the 1870s, the American inventor Thomas Edison made the first electric light bulb. Soon, Edison's "incandescent lamps" illuminated whole cities. The pace of city life quickened, and factories could continue to operate after dark. By the 1890s, cables carried electrical power from dynamos to factories.

New Methods of Production The basic features of the factory system remained the same during the 1800s. Factories still used large numbers of workers and power-driven machines to mass-produce goods. To improve efficiency, however, manufacturers designed products with interchangeable parts, identical components that could be used in place of one another. Interchangeable parts simplified both the assembly and repair of products.

By the early 1900s, manufacturers had introduced another new method of production, the assembly line. Workers on an assembly line add parts to a product that moves along a belt from one work station to the next. A different person performs each task along the assembly line. This division of labor in an assembly line, like interchangeable parts, made production faster and cheaper, lowering the price of goods. Although dividing labor into separate tasks proved to be more efficient, it took much of the joy out of the work itself.

✓ **Checkpoint** What was the dynamo's impact on the Industrial Revolution?

Electricity Lights Up Cities
This early dynamo (above) generated enough electricity to power lights in factories. Electricity changed life outdoors as well. *Judging from this print, how did electricity make life easier for people in the city?*

Unit 3: Reading and Taking Notes from Textbooks

Activity 3-2: The Preview Step (continued)

INFOGRAPHIC
The Modern Office

The Bessemer process prepared the way for the use of steel in building construction. Before steel, frameworks consisted of heavy iron. Steel provided a much lighter framework and enabled the construction of taller buildings. The first skyscrapers were between 10 and 20 stories high. They were built in the United States in the 1880s to house large corporations.

Elevators made it practical for buildings to have more than five or six stories.

Offices could be illuminated with **electric lights** both night and day.

Telephones allowed workers to send and receive messages faster than the telegraph.

Typewriters enabled workers to type information faster than they could write it by hand.

Automobiles and subway systems permitted rapid transit to and from cities.

ILLUSTRATION NOT TO SCALE

Thinking Critically
1. **Draw Inferences** Why did industrialization create a need for skyscrapers?
2. **Synthesize Information** What invention do you think had the most impact on offices? Explain.

302 Life in the Industrial Age

Transportation and Communication Advances

During the Industrial Revolution, transportation and communications were transformed by technology. Steamships replaced sailing ships, and railroad building took off. In Europe and North America, rail lines connected inland cities and seaports, mining regions and industrial centers. In the United States, a transcontinental railroad provided rail service from the Atlantic to the Pacific. In the same way, Russians built the Trans-Siberian Railroad, linking Moscow in European Russia to Vladivostok on the Pacific. Railroad tunnels and bridges crossed the Alps in Europe and the Andes in South America. Passengers and goods rode on rails in India, China, Egypt, and South Africa.

The Automobile Age Begins The transportation revolution took a new turn when a German engineer, Nikolaus Otto, invented a gasoline-powered internal combustion engine. In 1886, Karl Benz received a patent for the first automobile, which had three wheels. A year later, Gottlieb Daimler (DYM lur) introduced the first four-wheeled automobile. People laughed at the "horseless carriages," but they quickly transformed transportation.

The French nosed out the Germans as early automakers. Then the American Henry Ford started making models that reached the breathtaking speed of 25 miles per hour. In the early 1900s, Ford began using the assembly line to mass-produce cars, making the United States a leader in the automobile industry.

Airplanes Take Flight The internal combustion engine powered more than cars. Motorized threshers and reapers boosted farm production. Even more dramatically, the internal combustion engine made possible sustained, pilot-controlled flight. In 1903, American bicycle makers **Orville and Wilbur Wright** designed and flew a flimsy airplane at Kitty Hawk, North Carolina. Although their flying machine stayed aloft for only a few seconds, it ushered in the air age.

Soon, daredevil pilots were flying airplanes across the English Channel and over the Alps. Commercial passenger travel, however, would not begin until the 1920s.

Rapid Communication A revolution in communications also made the world smaller. An American inventor, Samuel F. B. Morse, developed

In 1901, Guglielmo Marconi (left) was in Newfoundland to receive the first overseas radio transmission from his assistant in England. Did Marconi's prediction come true? Explain.

Primary Source

"Shortly before mid-day I placed the single earphone to my ear and started listening.... I heard, faintly but distinctly, *pip-pip-pip*.... I now felt for the first time absolutely certain that the day would come when mankind would be able to send messages without wires not only across the Atlantic, but between the farthermost ends of the earth."

the telegraph, which could send coded messages over wires by means of electricity. His first telegraph line went into service between Washington, D.C. and Baltimore, in 1844. By the 1860s, an undersea cable was relaying messages between Europe and North America. This trans-Atlantic cable was an amazing engineering accomplishment for its day.

Communication soon became even faster. In 1876, the Scottish-born American inventor Alexander Graham Bell patented the telephone. By the 1890s, the Italian pioneer **Guglielmo Marconi** had invented the radio. In 1901, Marconi received a radio message, using Morse code, sent from Britain to Canada. Radio would become a cornerstone of today's global communications network.

✓ **Checkpoint** How did technological advances in transportation and communications affect the Industrial Revolution?

Business Takes a New Direction

By the late 1800s, what we call "big business" came to dominate industry. Big business refers to an establishment that is run by entrepreneurs who finance, manufacture, and distribute goods. As time passed, some big businesses came to control entire industries.

Rise of Big Business New technologies required the investment of large amounts of money, or capital. To get the needed capital, owners sold **stock,** or shares in their companies, to investors. Each stockholder became owner of a tiny part of a company. Large-scale companies, such as steel foundries, needed so much capital that they sold hundreds of thousands of shares. These businesses formed giant **corporations,** businesses that are owned by many investors who buy shares of stock. With large amounts of capital, corporations could expand into many areas.

Move Toward Monopolies Powerful business leaders created monopolies and trusts, huge corporate structures that controlled entire industries or areas of the economy. In Germany, Alfred Krupp inherited a steelmaking business from his father. He bought up coal and iron mines as well as ore deposits—supply lines or raw materials that fed the steel business. Later, he and his son acquired plants that made tools, railroad cars, and weapons. In the United States, John D. Rockefeller built Standard Oil Company into an empire. By gaining control of oil wells, oil refineries, and oil pipelines, he dominated the American petroleum industry.

Chapter 9 Section 1 303

Unit 3: Reading and Taking Notes from Textbooks

Activity 3-2: The Preview Step (continued)

Analyzing Political Cartoons

One View of Big Business To some critics, the growth of monopolies had a dangerous effect on society. This 1899 American cartoon shows a monopoly as an octopus-like monster. *Do you think this cartoonist favored or opposed government regulation of business? Explain.*

In their pursuit of profit, ruthless business leaders destroyed competing companies. With the competition gone, they were free to raise prices. Sometimes, a group of corporations would join forces and form a **cartel**, an association to fix prices, set production quotas, or control markets. In Germany, a single cartel fixed prices for 170 coal mines.

Move Toward Regulation The rise of big business and the creation of such great wealth sparked a stormy debate. Some people saw the Krupps and Rockefellers as "captains of industry" and praised their vision and skills. They pointed out that capitalists invested their wealth in worldwide ventures, such as railroad building, that employed thousands of workers and added to the general prosperity.

To others, the aggressive magnates were "robber barons." Destroying competition, critics argued, damaged the free-enterprise system, or the laissez-faire economy. Reformers called for laws to prevent monopolies and regulate large corporations. Despite questionable business practices, big business found support from many government leaders. By the early 1900s, some governments did move against monopolies. However, the political and economic power of business leaders often hindered efforts at regulation.

Checkpoint Why were big business leaders "captains of industry" to some, but "robber barons" to others?

SECTION 1 Assessment

Progress Monitoring Online
For: Self-quiz with vocabulary practice
Web Code: nba-2111

Terms, People, and Places
1. For each term, person, or place listed at the beginning of the section, write a sentence explaining its significance.

Note Taking
2. **Reading Skill: Identify Main Ideas** Use your completed chart to answer the Focus Question: How did science, technology, and big business promote industrial growth?

Comprehension and Critical Thinking
3. **Summarize** How did the Industrial Revolution spread in the 1800s?
4. **Draw Conclusions** How did technology help industry expand?
5. **Recognize Cause and Effect** How did the need for capital lead to new business organizations and methods?
6. **Predict** How might government change as a result of industrialization?

● **Writing About History**
Quick Write: Define a Problem Choose one topic from this section that you could use to write a problem-and-solution essay. For example, you could write about the impact of powerful monopolies. Make a list of details, facts, and examples that define the problems that monopolies pose to a free market.

304 Life in the Industrial Age

Unit 3: Reading and Taking Notes from Textbooks

Activity 3-2: The Preview Step (continued)

Answer the following questions based on your preview of Section 1.

1. What general idea about Section 1 did you learn from the title?

   _____

   _____

2. Was there an introduction to Section 1? _____

   If yes, what did the introduction alert you to expect?

   _____

   _____

3. Write each heading contained in Section 1.

   _____   _____

   _____   _____

   _____   _____

   _____   _____

   _____   _____

   _____   _____

   _____   _____

4. Based on the headings, write a summary statement that tells what you expect to learn by reading this section.

   _____

   _____

   _____

   _____

   _____

Unit 3: Reading and Taking Notes from Textbooks

Activity 3-2: The Preview Step (continued)

5. Did you get a better understanding of what Section 1 was about by looking at the visual aids and reading their titles or captions? _____

   If yes, how did the visual aids give you a better understanding of what Section 1 is about?

   _____

   _____

6. Was there a summary or conclusion at the end of Section 1? _____

   If yes, what did you learn about Section 1 from the summary or conclusion?

   _____

   _____

Activity 3-3: The Question, Read, and Write Steps

Question is the second step in the PQRW strategy. In this step use the words *who, what, where, when, why,* or *how* to change the first heading in the chapter or chapter part into a question to be answered. Write the question for the first heading in your notes using the format described in this activity. Sometimes it may be difficult to change the heading into a question. When this is the case, read the information that follows the heading and then write your question for that heading.

Read is the third step in the PQRW strategy. In this step read <u>all</u> of the information that follows the first heading. After reading all of the information, you may find that the question you wrote for the heading is not an appropriate question for that heading. If this happens, cross out the question you wrote and replace it with an appropriate question. You may also find that you should add one or more additional questions.

Write is the fourth step in the PQRW strategy. In this step write the answer to each question you wrote for the first heading. Include details to make the answer(s) as complete as possible.

Repeat the question, read, and write steps for each heading in the chapter or chapter part.

Here is the format you should use in your notebook when you use the PQRW strategy. Note that the format should not include "Title of Chapter Part" if a chapter is not divided into parts.

Complete the format for Section 1 of the chapter that was provided in Activity 3-2. The format is partially completed to help you get started.

Title of Textbook: World History

Title of Chapter: Life in the Industrial Age 1800-1914

Title of Chapter Part: The Industrial Revolution Spreads

Heading: New Industrial Powers Emerge

Question: What new industrial powers emerged?

Answer: Belgium followed by other nations challenged Britain's industrial supremacy.

Unit 3: Reading and Taking Notes from Textbooks

Activity 3-3: The Question, Read, and Write Steps (continued)

Heading: _____
Question: _____
Answer: _____
_____
_____

Heading: _____
Question: _____
Answer: _____
_____
_____

Heading: _____
Question: _____
Answer: _____
_____
_____

Heading: _____
Question: _____
Answer: _____
_____
_____

Unit 3: Reading and Taking Notes from Textbooks

Activity 3-3: The Question, Read, and Write Steps (continued)

Heading: _____
Question: _____
Answer: _____
_____
_____

Heading: _____
Question: _____
Answer: _____
_____
_____

Heading: _____
Question: _____
Answer: _____
_____
_____

Heading: _____
Question: _____
Answer: _____
_____
_____

Unit 3: Reading and Taking Notes from Textbooks

Activity 3-3: The Question, Read, and Write Steps (continued)

Heading: _____

Question: _____

Answer: _____

_____

_____

Heading: _____

Question: _____

Answer: _____

_____

_____

Heading: _____

Question: _____

Answer: _____

_____

_____

Heading: _____

Question: _____

Answer: _____

_____

_____

Unit 3: Reading and Taking Notes from Textbooks

Activity 3-3: The Question, Read, and Write Steps (continued)

Heading: _____
Question: _____
Answer: _____
_____
_____
_____

Heading: _____
Question: _____
Answer: _____
_____
_____
_____

Heading: _____
Question: _____
Answer: _____
_____
_____
_____

Heading: _____
Question: _____
Answer: _____
_____
_____
_____

Unit 3: Reading and Taking Notes from Textbooks

Activity 3-3: The Question, Read, and Write Steps (continued)

Heading: _____
Question: _____
Answer: _____
_____
_____
_____

Heading: _____
Question: _____
Answer: _____
_____
_____
_____

Heading: _____
Question: _____
Answer: _____
_____
_____
_____

Heading: _____
Question: _____
Answer: _____
_____
_____
_____

Unit 3: Reading and Taking Notes from Textbooks

Activity 3-4: Practice Using PQRW

Activity 3-4: Practice Using PQRW

Section 2, "The Rise of the Cities," appears on the pages that follow.

Complete the preview step of PQRW for Section 2. Then return to this page to answer the questions below.

1. What general idea about Section 2 did you learn from the title?

   _____

   _____

2. Was there an introduction to Section 2? _____

   If yes, what did the introduction alert you to expect?

   _____

   _____

3. Write each heading contained in Section 2.

   _____   _____

   _____   _____

   _____   _____

   _____   _____

   _____   _____

   _____   _____

   _____   _____

4. Based on the headings, write a summary statement that tells what you expect to learn by reading this section.

   _____

   _____

   _____

   _____

85

Copyright Mangrum-Strichart Learning Resources
www.mangrum-strichart.com

Unit 3: Reading and Taking Notes from Textbooks

Activity 3-4: Practice Using PQRW (continued)

5. Did you get a better understanding of what Section 2 is about by looking at the visual aids and reading their titles or captions? _____

   If yes, how did the visual aids give you a better understanding of what Section 2 is about?

   _____

   _____

6. Was there a summary or conclusion at the end of Section 2? _____

   If yes, what did you learn about Section 2 from the summary or conclusion?

   _____

   _____

WITNESS HISTORY 🔊 AUDIO
London Fog
Between 1850 and 1900, London's population more than doubled, rising from about 2.6 million people to more than 6.5 million people. With the rapid population growth came increased pollution and health problems:

❝ It was a foggy day in London, and the fog was heavy and dark. Animate [living] London, with smarting eyes and irritated lungs, was blinking, wheezing, and choking; inanimate [nonliving] London was a sooty spectre, divided in purpose between being visible and invisible, and so being wholly neither. ❞
—Charles Dickens, *Our Mutual Friend*

Charles Dickens with an illustration from one of his serialized novels

Focus Question How did the Industrial Revolution change life in the cities?

The Rise of the Cities

Objectives
- Summarize the impact of medical advances in the late 1800s.
- Describe how cities had changed by 1900.
- Explain how working-class struggles led to improved conditions for workers.

Terms, People, and Places
germ theory
Louis Pasteur
Robert Koch
Florence Nightingale
Joseph Lister
urban renewal
mutual-aid society
standard of living

Note Taking
Reading Skill: Identify Supporting Details As you read, look for the main ideas and supporting details and how they relate to each other. Use the format below to create an outline of the section.

```
I. Medicine and the population explosion
   A. The fight against disease
      1.
      2.
   B.
II.
```

The population explosion that had begun during the 1700s continued through the 1800s. Cities grew as rural people streamed into urban areas. By the end of the century, European and American cities had begun to take on many of the features of cities today.

Medicine Contributes to the Population Explosion
Between 1800 and 1900, the population of Europe more than doubled. This rapid growth was not due to larger families. In fact, families in most industrializing countries had fewer children. Instead, populations soared because the death rate fell. Nutrition improved, thanks in part to improved methods of farming, food storage, and distribution. Medical advances and improvements in public sanitation also slowed death rates.

The Fight Against Disease Since the 1600s, scientists had known of microscopic organisms, or microbes. Some scientists speculated that certain microbes might cause specific infectious diseases. Yet most doctors scoffed at this **germ theory**. Not until 1870 did French chemist **Louis Pasteur** (pas TUR) clearly show the link between microbes and disease. Pasteur went on to make other major contributions to medicine, including the development of vaccines against rabies and anthrax. He also discovered a process called pasteurization that killed disease-carrying microbes in milk.

Chapter 9 Section 2 305

BIOGRAPHY

Florence Nightingale

When Florence Nightingale (1820–1910) arrived at a British military hospital in the Crimea in 1854, she was horrified by what she saw. The sick and wounded lay on bare ground. With no sanitation and a shortage of food, some 60 percent of all patients died. But Nightingale was a fighter. Bullying the military and medical staff, she soon had every available person cleaning barracks, digging latrines, doing laundry, and caring for the wounded. Six months later, the death rate had dropped to 2 percent.

Back in England, Nightingale was hailed as a saint. Ballads were even written about her. She took advantage of her popularity and connections to pressure the government for reforms. **How did Nightingale achieve reforms in British army hospitals?**

In the 1880s, the German doctor **Robert Koch** identified the bacterium that caused tuberculosis, a respiratory disease that claimed about 30 million human lives in the 1800s. The search for a tuberculosis cure, however, took half a century. By 1914, yellow fever and malaria had been traced to microbes carried by mosquitoes.

As people understood how germs caused disease, they bathed and changed their clothes more often. In European cities, better hygiene helped decrease the rate of disease.

Hospital Care Improves In the early 1840s, anesthesia was first used to relieve pain during surgery. The use of anesthetics allowed doctors to experiment with operations that had never before been possible.

Yet, throughout the century, hospitals could be dangerous places. Surgery was performed with dirty instruments in dank rooms. Often, a patient would survive an operation, only to die days later of infection. For the poor, being admitted to a hospital was often a death sentence. Wealthy or middle-class patients insisted on treatment in their own homes.

"The very first requirement in a hospital," said British nurse **Florence Nightingale**, "is that it should do the sick no harm." As an army nurse during the Crimean War, Nightingale insisted on better hygiene in field hospitals. After the war, she worked to introduce sanitary measures in British hospitals. She also founded the world's first school of nursing.

The English surgeon **Joseph Lister** discovered how antiseptics prevented infection. He insisted that surgeons sterilize their instruments and wash their hands before operating. Eventually, the use of antiseptics drastically reduced deaths from infection.

✓ **Checkpoint** Which factors caused population rates to soar between 1800 and 1900?

City Life Changes

WITNESS HISTORY VIDEO

Watch *The Jungle: A View of Industrial America* on the **Witness History Discovery School**™ video program to learn more about city life during the industrial age.

Discovery SCHOOL

As industrialization progressed, cities came to dominate the West. City life, as old as civilization itself, underwent dramatic changes in Europe and the United States.

City Landscapes Change Growing wealth and industrialization altered the basic layout of European cities. City planners created spacious new squares and boulevards. They lined these avenues with government buildings, offices, department stores, and theaters.

The most extensive **urban renewal**, or rebuilding of the poor areas of a city, took place in Paris in the 1850s. Georges Haussmann, chief planner for Napoleon III, destroyed many tangled medieval streets full of tenement housing. In their place, he built wide boulevards and splendid public buildings. The project put many people to work, decreasing the threat of social

306 Life in the Industrial Age

unrest. The wide boulevards also made it harder for rebels to put up barricades and easier for troops to reach any part of the city.

Gradually, settlement patterns shifted. In most American cities, the rich lived in pleasant neighborhoods on the outskirts of the city. The poor crowded into slums near the city center, within reach of factories. Trolley lines made it possible to live in one part of the city and work in another.

Sidewalks, Sewers, and Skyscrapers Paved streets made urban areas much more livable. First gas lamps, and then electric street lights <u>illuminated</u> the night, increasing safety. Cities organized police forces and expanded fire protection.

Beneath the streets, sewage systems made cities much healthier places to live. City planners knew that clean water supplies and better sanitation methods were needed to combat epidemics of cholera and tuberculosis. In Paris, sewer lines expanded from 87 miles (139 kilometers) in 1852 to more than 750 miles (1200 kilometers) by 1911. The massive new sewer systems of London and Paris were costly, but they cut death rates dramatically.

By 1900, architects were using steel to construct soaring buildings. American architects like Louis Sullivan pioneered a new structure, the skyscraper. In large cities, single-family middle-class homes gave way to multistory apartment buildings.

Slum Conditions Despite efforts to improve cities, urban life remained harsh for the poor. Some working-class families could afford better clothing, newspapers, or tickets to a music hall. But they went home to small, cramped row houses or tenements in overcrowded neighborhoods.

In the worst tenements, whole families were often crammed into a single room. Unemployment or illness meant lost wages that could ruin a family. High rates of crime and alcoholism were a constant curse. Conditions had improved somewhat from the early Industrial Revolution, but slums remained a fact of city life.

Vocabulary Builder
<u>illuminate</u>—(ih LOO muh nayt) *v.* to light up; to give light to

Jacob Riis, a police reporter, photographer, and social activist in New York City published *How the Other Half Lives* in 1890 in an effort to expose the horrible living conditions of the city slums and tenements. Conditions among the urban working class in Britain (right) were similar to those in New York described by Riis:

Primary Source

"Look into any of these houses, everywhere the same .... Here is a "flat" or "parlor" and two pitch-dark coops called bedrooms.... One, two, three beds are there, if the old boxes and heaps of foul straw can be called by that name; a broken stove with crazy pipe from which the smoke leaks at every joint, a table of rough boards propped up on boxes, piles of rubbish in the corner. The closeness and smell are appalling. How many people sleep here? The woman with the red bandanna shakes her head sullenly, but the bare-legged girl with the bright face counts on her fingers... "Six, sir!""

Cause and Effect

Causes
- Increased agricultural productivity
- Growing population
- New sources of energy, such as steam and coal
- Growing demand for mass-produced goods
- Improved technology
- Available natural resources, labor, and money
- Strong, stable governments

Industrial Revolution

Immediate Effects
- Rise of factories
- Changes in transportation and communication
- Urbanization
- New methods of production
- Rise of urban working class
- Growth of reform movements

Long-Term Effects
- Growth of labor unions
- Inexpensive new products
- Increased pollution
- Rise of big business
- Expansion of public education
- Expansion of middle class
- Competition for world trade
- Progress in medical care

Connections to Today
- Improvements in world health
- Growth in population
- Industrialization in developing nations
- New energy sources, such as oil and nuclear power
- Environmental pollution
- Efforts to regulate world trade

Analyze Cause and Effect The long-term effects of the Industrial Revolution touched nearly every aspect of life. *Identify two social and two economic effects of the Industrial Revolution.*

The Lure of the City Despite their drawbacks, cities attracted millions. New residents were drawn as much by the excitement as by the promise of work. For tourists, too, cities were centers of action.

Music halls, opera houses, and theaters provided entertainment for every taste. Museums and libraries offered educational opportunities. Sports, from tennis to bare-knuckle boxing, drew citizens of all classes. Few of these enjoyments were available in country villages.

✓ **Checkpoint** How did industrialization change the face of cities?

The Working Class Advances

Workers tried to improve the harsh conditions of industrial life. They protested low wages, long hours, unsafe conditions, and the constant threat of unemployment. At first, business owners and governments tried to silence protesters. By mid-century, however, workers began to make progress.

Labor Unions Begin to Grow Workers formed **mutual-aid societies**, self-help groups to aid sick or injured workers. Men and women joined socialist parties or organized unions. The revolutions of 1830 and 1848 left vivid images of worker discontent, which governments could not ignore.

By the late 1800s, most Western countries had granted all men the vote. Workers also won the right to organize unions to bargain on their behalf. Germany legalized labor unions in 1869. Britain, Austria, and France followed. By 1900, Britain had about three million union members, and Germany had about two million. In France, membership grew from 140,000 in 1890 to over a million in 1912.

The main tactic of unions was the strike, or work stoppage. Workers used strikes to demand better working conditions, wage increases, or other benefits from their employers. Violence was often a result of strikes, particularly if employers tried to continue operating their businesses without the striking workers. Employers often called in the police to stop strikes.

Pressured by unions, reformers, and working-class voters, governments passed laws to regulate working conditions. Early laws forbade employers to hire children under the age of ten. Later, laws were passed outlawing child labor entirely and banning the employment of women in mines. Other laws limited work hours and improved safety. By 1909, British coal miners had won an eight-hour day, setting a standard for workers in other countries. In Germany, and then elsewhere, Western governments established old-age pensions, as well as disability insurance for workers who were hurt or became ill. These programs protected workers from poverty once they were no longer able to work.

308 Life in the Industrial Age

Unit 3: Reading and Taking Notes from Textbooks
Activity 3-4: Practice Using PQRW (continued)

Family Life and Leisure
With standards of living rising, families could pursue activities such as going to the movies. This 1896 French poster (left) advertises the Cinématographe Lumière (loom YEHR), the most successful motion-picture camera and projector of its day. *What does the clothing of the people in the poster suggest about their social rank?*

Standards of Living Rise Wages varied throughout the industrialized world, with unskilled laborers earning less than skilled workers. Women received less than half the pay of men doing the same work. Farm laborers barely scraped by during the economic slump of the late 1800s. Periods of unemployment brought desperate hardships to industrial workers and helped boost union membership.

Overall, though, standards of living for workers did rise. The standard of living measures the quality and availability of necessities and comforts in a society. Families ate more varied diets, lived in better homes, and dressed in inexpensive, mass-produced clothing. Advances in medicine improved health. Some workers moved to the suburbs, traveling to work on subways and trolleys. Still, the gap between workers and the middle class widened.

✓ **Checkpoint** How did workers try to improve their living and working conditions?

SECTION 2 Assessment

Progress Monitoring Online
For: Self-quiz with vocabulary practice
Web Code: nba-2121

Terms, People, and Places
1. For each term, person, or place listed at the beginning of the section, write a sentence explaining its significance.

Note Taking
2. **Reading Skill: Identify Supporting Details** Use your completed outline to answer the Focus Question: How did the Industrial Revolution change life in the cities?

Comprehension and Critical Thinking
3. **Recognize Cause and Effect** Why did the rate of population growth increase in the late 1800s?
4. **Summarize** What are three ways that city life changed in the 1800s?
5. **Analyze Information** What laws helped workers in the late 1800s?
6. **Synthesize Information** How did the rise of the cities challenge the economic and social order of the time?

● **Writing About History**
Quick Write: Brainstorm Possible Solutions Choose one topic from this section, such as the hardships of city life, about which you could write a problem-solution essay. Use the text and your own knowledge to create a list of possible solutions to the problem that you've chosen to write about. Next, organize your list to rank the solutions from most effective to least effective.

Chapter 9 Section 2   309

Unit 3: Reading and Taking Notes from Textbooks

Activity 3-4: Practice Using PQRW (continued)

Now, complete the question, read, and write steps of PQRW for Section 2.

Title of Textbook: _____

Title of Chapter: _____

Title of Chapter Part: _____

Heading: _____

Question: _____

Answer: _____
_____
_____
_____

Heading: _____

Question: _____

Answer: _____
_____
_____
_____

Heading: _____

Question: _____

Answer: _____
_____
_____
_____

Unit 3: Reading and Taking Notes from Textbooks

Activity 3-4: Practice Using PQRW (continued)

Heading: _____
Question: _____
Answer: _____
_____
_____

Heading: _____
Question: _____
Answer: _____
_____
_____

Heading: _____
Question: _____
Answer: _____
_____
_____

Heading: _____
Question: _____
Answer: _____
_____
_____

Unit 3: Reading and Taking Notes from Textbooks

Activity 3-4: Practice Using PQRW (continued)

Heading: _____
Question: _____
Answer: _____
_____
_____
_____

Heading: _____
Question: _____
Answer: _____
_____
_____
_____

Heading: _____
Question: _____
Answer: _____
_____
_____
_____

Heading: _____
Question: _____
Answer: _____
_____
_____
_____

Unit 3: Reading and Taking Notes from Textbooks

Activity 3-4: Practice Using PQRW (continued)

Heading: _____
Question: _____
Answer: _____
_____
_____

Heading: _____
Question: _____
Answer: _____
_____
_____

Heading: _____
Question: _____
Answer: _____
_____
_____

Unit 3: Reading and Taking Notes from Textbooks

Activity 3-5: Practice Using PQRW

Activity 3-5: Practice Using PQRW

Section 3, "Changing Attitudes and Values" appears on the pages that follow.

Complete the preview step of PQRW for Section 3. Then return to this page to answer the questions below.

1. What general idea about Section 3 did you learn from the title?

   _____

   _____

2. Was there an introduction to Section 3? _____

   If yes, what did the introduction alert you to expect?

   _____

   _____

3. Write each heading contained in Section 3.

   _____   _____

   _____   _____

   _____   _____

   _____   _____

   _____   _____

   _____   _____

   _____   _____

4. Based on the headings, write a summary statement that tells what you expect to learn by reading this section.

   _____

   _____

   _____

   _____

   _____

Unit 3: Reading and Taking Notes from Textbooks

Activity 3-5: Practice Using PQRW (continued)

5. After reading the headings, what specific information did you expect to find in Section 3?

   _____

   _____

6. Did you get a better understanding of what Section 3 is about by looking at the visual aids and reading their titles or captions? _____

   If yes, how did the visual aids give you a better understanding of what Section 3 is about?

   _____

   _____

7. Was there a summary or conclusion at the end of Section 3? _____

   If yes, what did you learn about Section 3 from the summary or conclusion?

   _____

   _____

Unit 3: Reading and Taking Notes from Textbooks
Activity 3-5: Practice Using PQRW (continued)

Suffragette arrested in London, 1914

Women's suffrage banner

WITNESS HISTORY AUDIO
Votes for Women
After years of peacefully protesting the British government's refusal to allow women to vote, some activists turned to confrontation:

❝We have been driven to the conclusion that only through legislation can any improvement be effected, and that that legislation can never be effected until we have the same power as men have to bring pressure to bear upon our representatives and upon Governments to give us the necessary legislation.... We are here not because we are law-breakers; we are here in our efforts to become law-makers.❞
—Emmeline Pankhurst, October 21, 1908

Focus Question How did the Industrial Revolution change the old social order and long-held traditions in the Western world?

Changing Attitudes and Values

Objectives
- Explain what values shaped the new social order.
- Understand how women and educators sought change.
- Learn how science challenged existing beliefs.

Terms, People, and Places

cult of domesticity	John Dalton
temperance movement	Charles Darwin
Elizabeth Cady Stanton	racism
women's suffrage	social gospel
Sojourner Truth	

Note Taking

Reading Skill: Identify Supporting Details As you read, create a table listing new attitudes and values in the left-hand column. List the supporting details in the right-hand column.

Changes in Social Order and Values	
Issue	Change
• New social order	•
• Rights for women	•
•	•

312 Life in the Industrial Age

Demand for women's rights was one of many issues that challenged the traditional social order in the late 1800s. By then, in many countries, the middle class—aspiring to upper-class wealth and privilege—increasingly came to dominate society.

A New Social Order Arises
The Industrial Revolution slowly changed the social order in the Western world. For centuries, the two main classes were nobles and peasants. Their roles were defined by their relationship to the land. While middle-class merchants, artisans, and lawyers played important roles, they still had a secondary position in society. With the spread of industry, a more complex social structure emerged.

Three Social Classes Emerge By the late 1800s, Western Europe's new upper class included very rich business families. Wealthy entrepreneurs married into aristocratic families, gaining the status of noble titles. Nobles needed the money brought by the industrial rich to support their lands and lifestyle.

Below this tiny elite, a growing middle class was pushing its way up the social ladder. Its highest rungs were filled with mid-level business people and professionals such as doctors and scientists. With comfortable incomes, they enjoyed a wide range of material goods. Next came the lower middle class, which included teachers and office workers. They struggled to keep up with their "betters."

98

Copyright Mangrum-Strichart Learning Resources
www.mangrum-strichart.com

Workers and peasants were at the base of the social ladder. In highly industrialized Britain, workers made up more than 30 percent of the population in 1900. In Western Europe and the United States, the number of farmworkers dropped, but many families still worked the land. The rural population was higher in eastern and southern Europe, where industrialization was more limited.

Middle-Class Tastes and Values By mid-century, the modern middle class had developed its own way of life. A strict code of etiquette governed social behavior. Rules dictated how to dress for every occasion, how to give a dinner party, how to pay a social call, when to write letters, and how long to mourn for dead relatives.

Parents strictly supervised their children, who were expected to be "seen but not heard." A child who misbehaved was considered to reflect badly on the entire family. Servants, too, were seen as a reflection of their employers. Even a small middle-class household was expected to have at least a cook and a housemaid.

The Ideal Home Within the family, the division of labor between wife and husband changed. Earlier, middle-class women had helped run family businesses out of the home. By the later 1800s, most middle-class husbands went to work in an office or shop. A successful husband was one who earned enough to keep his wife at home. Women spent their time raising children, directing servants, and doing religious or charitable service.

Books, magazines, and popular songs supported a cult of domesticity that idealized women and the home. Sayings like "home, sweet home" were stitched into needlework and hung on parlor walls. The ideal woman was seen as a tender, self-sacrificing caregiver who provided a nest for her children and a peaceful refuge for her husband to escape from the hardships of the working world.

This ideal rarely applied to the lower classes. Working-class women labored for low pay in garment factories or worked as domestic servants. Young women might leave domestic service after they married, but often had to seek other employment. Despite long days working for wages, they were still expected to take full responsibility for child care and homemaking.

✓ **Checkpoint** How had the social order changed by the late 1800s?

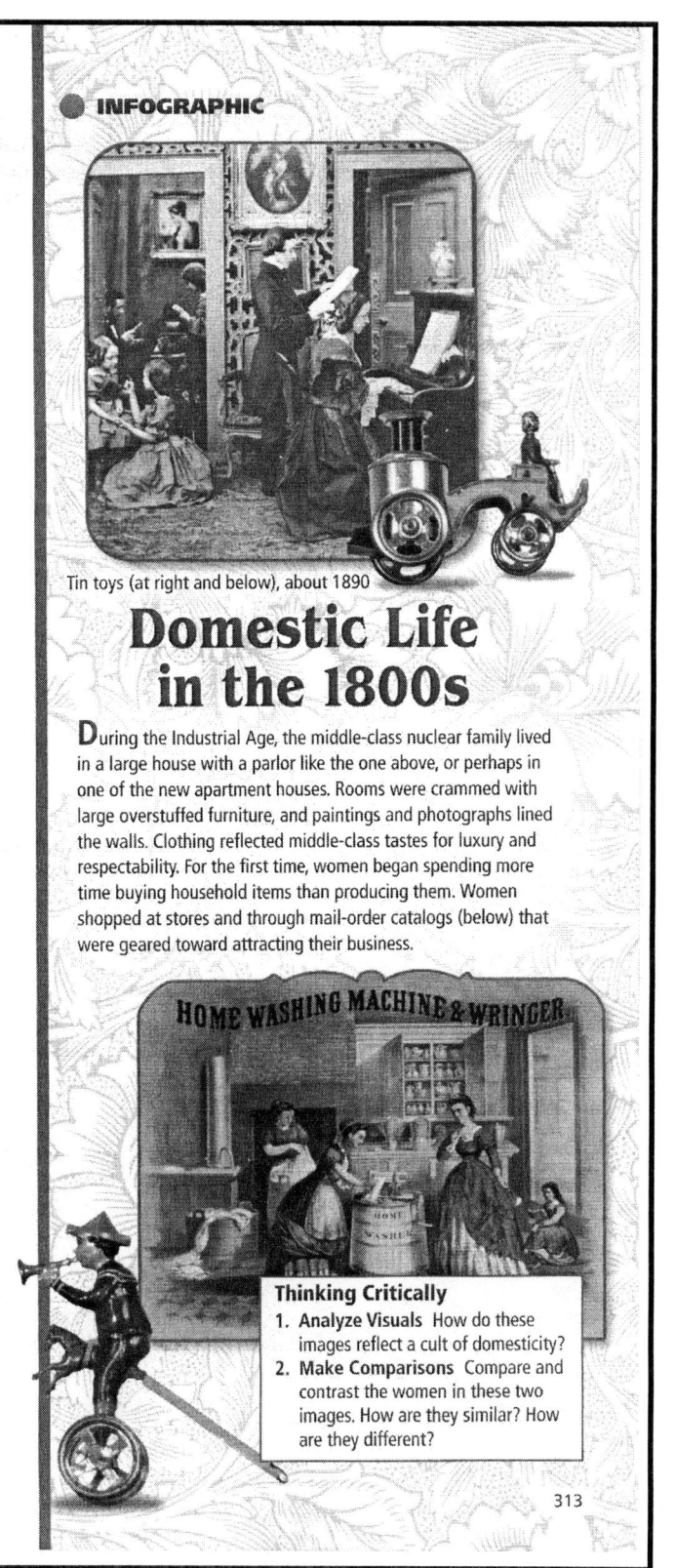

● **INFOGRAPHIC**

Tin toys (at right and below), about 1890

Domestic Life in the 1800s

During the Industrial Age, the middle-class nuclear family lived in a large house with a parlor like the one above, or perhaps in one of the new apartment houses. Rooms were crammed with large overstuffed furniture, and paintings and photographs lined the walls. Clothing reflected middle-class tastes for luxury and respectability. For the first time, women began spending more time buying household items than producing them. Women shopped at stores and through mail-order catalogs (below) that were geared toward attracting their business.

Thinking Critically
1. **Analyze Visuals** How do these images reflect a cult of domesticity?
2. **Make Comparisons** Compare and contrast the women in these two images. How are they similar? How are they different?

Unit 3: Reading and Taking Notes from Textbooks

Activity 3-5: Practice Using PQRW (continued)

In an 1892 address, the American women's rights leader Elizabeth Cady Stanton argued that women should have an equal right to education. How does Stanton believe that an education would help women better control their own lives?

Primary Source

"... As an individual, she must rely on herself. ... To throw obstacles in the way of a complete education is like putting out the eyes. ... In talking of education, how shallow the argument that [men and women] must be educated for the special work [they propose] to do, and that all of the faculties not needed in this special work must lie dormant and utterly wither for lack of use, when, perhaps, these will be the very faculties needed in life's greatest emergencies!" — "The Solitude of Self"

African American suffragist Sojourner Truth

314

Women Work for Rights

Some individual women and women's groups protested restrictions on women. They sought a broad range of rights. Across Europe and the United States, politically active women campaigned for fairness in marriage, divorce, and property laws. Women's groups also supported the **temperance movement**, a campaign to limit or ban the use of alcoholic beverages. Temperance leaders argued not only that drinking threatened family life, but that banning it was important for a productive and efficient workforce.

These reformers faced many obstacles. In Europe and the United States, women could not vote. They were barred from most schools and had little, if any, protection under the law. A woman's husband or father controlled all of her property.

Early Voices Before 1850, some women—mostly from the middle class—had campaigned for the abolition of slavery. In the process, they realized the severe restrictions on their own lives. In the United States, Lucretia Mott, **Elizabeth Cady Stanton**, and Susan B. Anthony crusaded against slavery before organizing a movement for women's rights.

Many women broke the barriers that kept them out of universities and professions. By the late 1800s, a few women trained as doctors or lawyers. Others became explorers, researchers, or inventors, often without recognition. For example, Julia Brainerd Hall worked with her brother to develop an aluminum-producing process. Their company became hugely successful, but Charles Hall received almost all of the credit.

The Suffrage Struggle By the late 1800s, married women in some countries had won the right to control their own property. The struggle for political rights proved far more difficult. In the United States, the Seneca Falls Convention of 1848 demanded that women be granted the right to vote. In Europe, groups dedicated to **women's suffrage**, or women's right to vote, emerged in the later 1800s.

Among men, some liberals and socialists supported women's suffrage. In general, though, suffragists faced intense opposition. Some critics claimed that women were too emotional to be allowed to vote. Others argued that women needed to be "protected" from grubby politics or that a woman's place was in the home, not in government. To such claims, **Sojourner Truth**, an African American suffragist, is believed to have replied, "Nobody ever helps me into carriages, or over mudpuddles, or gives me any best place! And ain't I a woman?"

On the edges of the Western world, women made faster strides. In New Zealand, Australia, and some western territories of the United States, women won the vote by the early 1900s. There, women who had "tamed the frontier" alongside men were not dismissed as weak and helpless. In the United States, Wyoming became the first state to grant women the right to vote. In Europe and most of the United States, however, the suffrage struggle succeeded only after World War I.

✓ **Checkpoint** What were the arguments against women's suffrage?

Growth of Public Education

By the late 1800s, reformers persuaded many governments to set up public schools and require basic education for all children. Teaching "the three Rs"—reading, writing, and 'rithmetic—was thought to produce better citizens. In addition, industrialized societies recognized the need for a literate workforce. Schools taught punctuality, obedience to authority, disciplined work habits, and patriotism. In European schools, children also received basic religious education.

Public Education Improves At first, elementary schools were primitive. Many teachers had little schooling themselves. In rural areas, students attended class only during the times when they were not needed on the farm or in their parents' shops.

By the late 1800s, more and more children were in school, and the quality of elementary education improved. Teachers received training at Normal Schools, where the latest "norms and standards" of educational practices were taught. Beginning in 1879, schools to train teachers were established in France. In England, schooling girls and boys between the ages of five and ten became compulsory after 1881. Also, governments began to expand secondary schools, known as high schools in the United States. In secondary schools, students learned the "classical languages," Latin and Greek, along with history and mathematics.

In general, only middle-class families could afford to have their sons attend these schools, which trained students for more serious study or for government jobs. Middle-class girls were sent to school primarily in the hope that they might marry well and become better wives and mothers. Education for girls did not include subjects such as science, mathematics, or physical education because they were not seen as necessary subjects for girls to learn.

Higher Education Expands Colleges and universities expanded in this period, too. Most university students were the sons of middle- or upper-class families. The university curriculum emphasized ancient history and languages, philosophy, religion, and law. By the late 1800s, universities added courses in the sciences, especially in chemistry and physics. At the same time, engineering schools trained students who would have the knowledge and skills to build the new industrial society.

Some women sought greater educational opportunities. By the 1840s, a few small colleges for women opened, including Bedford College in England and Mount Holyoke in the United States. In 1863, the British reformer Emily Davies campaigned for female students to be allowed to take the entrance examinations for Cambridge University. She succeeded, but as late as 1897, male Cambridge students rioted against granting degrees to women.

✓ **Checkpoint** Why did more children attend school in the late 1800s than before?

Public Education
Before 1870, the only formal education available for British children was in religious schools or "ragged schools," which taught poor children basic skills, such as reading. The Industrial Revolution changed that as it created a growing need for people to be better educated. *How does this 1908 photo of a science class in London illustrate the changes that had taken place in the British educational system?*

Unit 3: Reading and Taking Notes from Textbooks

Activity 3-5: Practice Using PQRW (continued)

Science Takes New Directions

Science in the service of industry brought great changes in the later 1800s. At the same time, researchers advanced startling theories about the natural world. Their new ideas challenged long-held beliefs.

Atomic Theory Develops A crucial breakthrough in chemistry came in the early 1800s when the English Quaker schoolteacher John Dalton developed modern atomic theory. The ancient Greeks had speculated that all matter was made of tiny particles called atoms. Dalton showed that each element has its own kind of atoms. Earlier theories put forth the idea that all atoms were basically alike. Dalton also showed how different kinds of atoms combine to make all chemical substances. In 1869, the Russian chemist Dmitri Mendeleyev (men duh LAY ef) drew up a table that grouped elements according to their atomic weights. His table became the basis for the periodic table of elements used today.

Debating the Earth's Age The new science of geology opened avenues of debate. In *Principles of Geology*, Charles Lyell offered evidence to

Vocabulary Builder
speculate—(SPEK yuh layt) *v.* to think about

INFOGRAPHIC

In 1831, the HMS *Beagle* sailed from England on a five-year voyage around the world to survey and chart the oceans. Aboard was 22-year-old Charles Darwin, whose role was to observe, record, and collect samples of rocks, plants, animals, insects, and fossils. Some of the animals that he studied are pictured on the map. The specimens Darwin collected and studied helped him develop his theory of evolution. Controversy over Darwin's theory continues today.

▶ Clockwise from upper right: blue common Morpho butterfly, bottlenose dolphin, jaguar, Galápagos tortoise

Voyage of the HMS *Beagle*

316 Life in the Industrial Age

show that Earth had formed over millions of years. His successors concluded that Earth was at least two billion years old and that life had not appeared until long after Earth was formed. These ideas did not seem to agree with biblical accounts of creation.

Archaeology added other pieces to an emerging debate about the origins of life on Earth. In 1856, workers in Germany accidentally uncovered fossilized Neanderthal bones. Later scholars found fossils of other early modern humans. These archaeologists had limited evidence and often drew mistaken conclusions. But as more discoveries were made, scholars developed new ideas about early humans and their ancestors.

Darwin's Theory of Natural Selection The most controversial new idea came from the British naturalist **Charles Darwin**. In 1859, after years of research, he published *On the Origin of Species*. Darwin argued that all forms of life, including human beings, had evolved into their present state over millions of years. To explain the long, slow process of evolution, he put forward his theory of natural selection.

Darwin adopted Thomas Malthus's idea that all plants and animals produced more offspring than the food supply could support. As a result,

Vocabulary Builder
controversial—(kahn truh VUR shul) *adj.* that is or can be argued about or debated

These four species of finches from the Galápagos Islands have different beaks and eating habits. Darwin (above) theorized that isolation, plus time, and adapting to local conditions, leads to new species.

From top to bottom: black-browed albatross, pink cockatoo, flying fish

History Interactive
For: Interactive map, audio, and more
Web Code: nba-4174

Thinking Critically
1. **Draw Conclusions** How did Darwin's voyage help him develop his theory of natural selection?
2. **Synthesize Information** Why would the isolation of Galápagos Islands attract scientists such as Darwin?

Chapter 9 Section 3 317

Unit 3: Reading and Taking Notes from Textbooks

Activity 3-5: Practice Using PQRW (continued)

he said, members of each species constantly competed to survive. Natural forces "selected" those with physical traits best adapted to their environment to survive and to pass the trait on to their offspring. This process of natural selection came to be known as "survival of the fittest."

Social Darwinism and Racism Although Darwin himself never promoted any social ideas, some thinkers used his theories to support their own beliefs about society. Applying the idea of survival of the fittest to war and economic competition came to be known as Social Darwinism. Industrial tycoons, argued Social Darwinists, were more "fit" than those they put out of business. War brought progress by weeding out weak nations. Victory was seen as proof of superiority.

Social Darwinism encouraged racism, the unscientific belief that one racial group is superior to another. By the late 1800s, many Europeans and Americans claimed that the success of Western civilization was due to the supremacy of the white race. As you will read, such powerful ideas would have a long-lasting impact on world history.

✓ **Checkpoint** How did science begin to challenge existing beliefs in the late 1800s?

Religion in an Urban Age

Despite the challenge of new scientific ideas, religion continued to be a major force in Western society. Christian churches and Jewish synagogues remained at the center of communities. Religious leaders influenced political, social, and educational developments.

The grim realities of industrial life stimulated feelings of compassion and charity. Christian labor unions and political parties pushed for reforms. Individuals, church groups, and Jewish organizations all tried to help the working poor. Catholic priests and nuns set up schools and hospitals in urban slums. Many Protestant churches backed the social gospel, a movement that urged Christians to social service. They campaigned for reforms in housing, healthcare, and education.

✓ **Checkpoint** How did religious groups respond to the challenges of industrialization?

The Salvation Army
By 1878, William and Catherine Booth had set up the Salvation Army in London to spread Christian teachings and provide social services. Their daughter, Evangeline (below), stands in front of one the kettles used to gather funds for the needy. *What services did religious organizations provide?*

Section 3 Assessment

Progress Monitoring Online
For: Self-quiz with vocabulary practice
Web Code: nba-2131

Terms, People, and Places
1. For each term, person, or place listed at the beginning of the section, write a sentence explaining its significance.

Note Taking
2. **Reading Skill: Identify Supporting Details** Use your completed table to answer the Focus Question: How did the Industrial Revolution change the old social order and long-held traditions in the Western world?

Comprehension and Critical Thinking
3. **Describe** What are three values associated with the middle class?
4. **Draw Conclusions** Why did the women's movement face strong opposition?
5. **Draw Inferences** Why do you think reformers pushed for free public education?
6. **Synthesize Information** Why did the ideas of Charles Darwin cause controversy?

● **Writing About History**
Quick Write: Write a Thesis Statement Imagine that you are writing a problem-solution essay on the unequal treatment of women in the 1800s. Based on what you have read in this section, write a thesis statement, or the main idea, for your problem-solution essay.

318 Life in the Industrial Age

Unit 3: Reading and Taking Notes from Textbooks
Activity 3-5: Practice Using PQRW (continued)

Now, complete the question, read, and write steps of PQRW for Section 3.

Title of Textbook: _____

Title of Chapter: _____

Title of Chapter Part: _____

Heading: _____

Question: _____

Answer: _____

_____

_____

Heading: _____

Question: _____

Answer: _____

_____

_____

Heading: _____

Question: _____

Answer: _____

_____

_____

Unit 3: Reading and Taking Notes from Textbooks
Activity 3-5: Practice Using PQRW (continued)

Heading: _____
Question: _____
Answer: _____
_____
_____
_____

Heading: _____
Question: _____
Answer: _____
_____
_____
_____

Heading: _____
Question: _____
Answer: _____
_____
_____
_____

Heading: _____
Question: _____
Answer: _____
_____
_____
_____

Unit 3: Reading and Taking Notes from Textbooks

Activity 3-5: Practice Using PQRW (continued)

Heading: _____
Question: _____
Answer: _____
_____
_____

Heading: _____
Question: _____
Answer: _____
_____
_____

Heading: _____
Question: _____
Answer: _____
_____
_____

Heading: _____
Question: _____
Answer: _____
_____
_____

Unit 3: Reading and Taking Notes from Textbooks

Activity 3-5: Practice Using PQRW (continued)

Heading: _____
Question: _____
Answer: _____
_____
_____

Heading: _____
Question: _____
Answer: _____
_____
_____

Heading: _____
Question: _____
Answer: _____
_____
_____

Heading: _____
Question: _____
Answer: _____
_____
_____

Unit 3: Reading and Taking Notes from Textbooks

Activity 3-5: Practice Using PQRW (continued)

Heading: _____
Question: _____
Answer: _____
_____
_____

Heading: _____
Question: _____
Answer: _____
_____
_____

Heading: _____
Question: _____
Answer: _____
_____
_____

Heading: _____
Question: _____
Answer: _____
_____
_____

Unit 3: Reading and Taking Notes from Textbooks

Activity 3-5: Practice Using PQRW (continued)

Heading: _____
Question: _____
Answer: _____
_____
_____
_____

Heading: _____
Question: _____
Answer: _____
_____
_____
_____

Heading: _____
Question: _____
Answer: _____
_____
_____
_____

Heading: _____
Question: _____
Answer: _____
_____
_____
_____

Unit 3: Reading and Taking Notes from Textbooks

Activity 3-6: Practice Using PQRW

Activity 3-6: Practice Using PQRW

Section 4, "Arts in the Industrial Age," appears on the pages that follow.

Complete the preview step of PQRW for Section 4. Then return to this page to answer the questions below.

1. What general idea about Section 4 did you learn from the title?

   _____

   _____

2. Was there an introduction to Section 4? _____

   If yes, what did the introduction alert you to expect?

   _____

   _____

3. Write each heading contained in Section 4.

   _____   _____

   _____   _____

   _____   _____

   _____   _____

   _____   _____

   _____   _____

4. Based on the headings, write a summary statement that tells what you expect to learn by reading this section.

   _____

   _____

   _____

   _____

   _____

Unit 3: Reading and Taking Notes from Textbooks

Activity 3-6: Practice Using PQRW (continued)

5. Did you get a better understanding of what Section 4 is about by looking at the visual aids and reading their titles or captions? _____

   If yes, how did the visual aids give you a better understanding of what Section 4 is about?

   _____

   _____

6. Was there a summary or conclusion at the end of Section 4? _____

   If yes, what did you learn about Section 4 from the summary or conclusion?

   _____

   _____

Albert Bierstadt, *Hetch Hetchy Canyon*, 1875

Arts in the Industrial Age

WITNESS HISTORY 🔊 AUDIO
Sunset
In the 1800s, many writers turned away from the harsh realities of industrial life to celebrate nature. The English poet William Wordsworth described the peace and beauty of sunset:

❝ It is a beauteous evening, calm and free,
The holy time is quiet as a Nun
Breathless with adoration; the broad sun
Is sinking down in its tranquillity. ❞
—William Wordsworth,
Complete Poetical Works

Focus Question What artistic movements emerged in reaction to the Industrial Revolution?

Objectives
- Understand what themes shaped romantic art, literature, and music.
- Explain how realists responded to the industrialized, urban world.
- Describe how the visual arts changed.

Terms, People, and Places

William Wordsworth	realism
William Blake	Charles Dickens
romanticism	Gustave Courbet
Lord Byron	Louis Daguerre
Victor Hugo	impressionism
Ludwig van Beethoven	Claude Monet
	Vincent van Gogh

Note Taking
Reading Skill: Identify Supporting Details Fill in a table like the one below with details about the artistic movements in the 1800s.

Major Artistic Movements of the 1800s		
Movement	Goals/ Characteristics	Major Figures
Romanticism	• Rebellion against reason	• Wordsworth
Realism	•	•
Impressionism	•	•

William Wordsworth, along with William Blake, Samuel Taylor Coleridge, and Percy Bysshe Shelley among others, was part of a cultural movement called romanticism. From about 1750 to 1850, romanticism shaped Western literature and arts.

The Romantic Revolt Against Reason
Romanticism does not refer to romance in the sense of an affectionate relationship, but rather to an artistic style emphasizing imagination, freedom, and emotion. Romanticism was a reaction to the neoclassical writers of the Enlightenment, who had turned to classical Greek and Roman literature and ideals that stressed order, harmony, reason, and emotional restraint. In contrast to Enlightenment literature, the works of romantic writers included simple, direct language, intense feelings, and a glorification of nature. Artists, composers, and architects were also followers of the movement.

The Romantic Hero Romantic writers created a new kind of hero—a mysterious, melancholy figure who felt out of step with society. "My joys, my grief, my passions, and my powers, / Made me a stranger," wrote Britain's George Gordon, **Lord Byron**. He himself was a larger-than-life figure equal to those he created. After a rebellious, wandering life, he joined Greek forces battling for freedom. When he died of a fever there, his legend bloomed. In fact, public interest in his poetry and adventures was so great that moody, isolated romantic heroes came to be described as "Byronic."

Chapter 9 Section 4 319

BIOGRAPHY

Ludwig van Beethoven

An accomplished musician by age 12, composer Ludwig van Beethoven (1770–1827) agonized over every note of every composition. The result was stunning music that expresses intense emotion. The famous opening of his Fifth Symphony conveys the sense of fate knocking at the door. His Sixth Symphony captures a joyful day in the countryside, interrupted by a violent thunderstorm.

Beethoven's career was haunted by perhaps the greatest tragedy a musician can face. In 1798, he began to lose his hearing. Still, he continued to compose music he could hear only in his mind. **How did Beethoven's music reflect romanticism?**

🔊 AUDIO

The romantic hero often hid a guilty secret and faced a grim destiny. German writer Johann Wolfgang von Goethe (GUR tuh) wrote the dramatic poem *Faust*. The aging scholar Faust makes a pact with the devil, exchanging his soul for youth. After much agony, Faust wins salvation by accepting his duty to help others. In *Jane Eyre*, British novelist Charlotte Brontë weaves a tale about a quiet governess and her brooding, Byronic employer, whose large mansion conceals a terrifying secret.

Inspired by the Past Romantic writers combined history, legend, and folklore. Sir Walter Scott's novels and ballads evoked the turbulent history of Scottish clans or medieval knights. Alexandre Dumas (doo MAH) and **Victor Hugo** re-created France's past in novels like *The Three Musketeers* and *The Hunchback of Notre Dame*.

Architects, too, were inspired by old styles and forms. Churches and other buildings, including the British Parliament, were modeled on medieval Gothic styles. To people living in the 1800s, medieval towers and lacy stonework conjured up images of a glorious past.

Music Stirs Emotions Romantic composers also tried to stir deep emotions. Audiences were moved to laughter or tears at Hungarian Franz Liszt's piano playing. The passionate music of German composer **Ludwig van Beethoven** combined classical forms with a stirring range of sound. He was the first composer to take full advantage of the broad range of instruments in the modern orchestra. In all, Beethoven produced nine symphonies, five piano concertos, a violin concerto, an opera, two masses, and dozens of shorter pieces. To many, he is considered the greatest composer of his day.

Other romantic composers wove traditional folk melodies into their works to glorify their nations' pasts. In his piano works, Frederic Chopin (shoh PAN) used Polish peasant dances to convey the sorrows and joys of people living under foreign occupation.

Romanticism in Art Painters, too, broke free from the discipline and strict rules of the Enlightenment. Landscape painters like J.M.W. Turner sought to capture the beauty and power of nature. Using bold brush strokes and colors, Turner often showed tiny human figures struggling against sea and storm.

Romantics painted many subjects, from simple peasant life to medieval knights to current events. Bright colors conveyed violent energy and emotion. The French painter Eugène Delacroix (deh luh KRWAH) filled his canvases with dramatic action. In *Liberty Leading the People*, the Goddess of Liberty carries the revolutionary tricolor as French citizens rally to the cause.

✓ **Checkpoint** How did romantic writers, musicians, and artists respond to the Enlightenment?

The Call to Realism

By the mid-1800s, a new artistic movement, realism, took hold in the West. Realism was an attempt to represent the world as it was, without the sentiment associated with romanticism. Realists often focused their work on the harsh side of life in cities or villages. Many writers and artists were committed to improving the lot of the unfortunates whose lives they depicted.

320 Life in the Industrial Age

Novels Depict Grim Reality The English novelist Charles Dickens vividly portrayed the lives of slum dwellers and factory workers, including children. In *Oliver Twist,* Dickens tells the story of a nine-year-old orphan raised in a grim poorhouse. In response to a request for more food, Oliver is smacked on the head and sent away to work. Later, he runs away to London. There he is taken in by Fagin, a villain who trains homeless children to become pickpockets. The book shocked many middle-class readers with its picture of poverty, mistreatment of children, and urban crime. Yet Dickens's humor and colorful characters made him one of the most popular novelists in the world.

French novelists also portrayed the ills of their time. Victor Hugo, who moved from romantic to realistic novels, revealed how hunger drove a good man to crime and how the law hounded him ever after in *Les Misérables* (lay miz ehr AHB). The novels of Émile Zola painted an even grimmer picture. In *Germinal,* Zola exposed class warfare in the French mining industry. To Zola's characters, neither the Enlightenment's faith in reason nor the romantic movement's feelings mattered at all.

Realism in Drama Norwegian dramatist Henrik Ibsen brought realism to the stage. His plays attacked the hypocrisy he observed around him. *A Doll's House* shows a woman caught in a straitjacket of social rules. In *An Enemy of the People,* a doctor discovers that the water in a local spa is polluted. Because the town's economy depends on its spa, the citizens denounce the doctor and suppress the truth. Ibsen's realistic dramas had a wide influence in Europe and the United States.

Realism in the Arts

(A) Thomas Eakins's 1875 painting *The Gross Clinic* depicts the realism of medical school where students learn by performing autopsies. The artist included many realistic elements such as the surgical tools in the foreground and the reaction of the spectator at the far left.

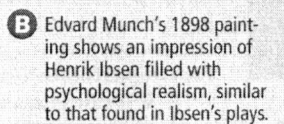

(B) Edvard Munch's 1898 painting shows an impression of Henrik Ibsen filled with psychological realism, similar to that found in Ibsen's plays.

(C) This 1896 portrait of Ibsen shows photographic realism in the playwright's appearance and expression.

(D) Victor Hugo's 1862 novel *Les Misérables* describes the reality of poverty, hunger, and corruption among the poor in Paris. This 1886 poster depicts the novel's main characters: the convict Jean Valjean at the center, and Cosette, the girl he adopts, at the right.

Arts Reject Romantic Ideas Painters also represented the realities of their time. Rejecting the romantic <u>emphasis</u> on imagination, they focused on ordinary subjects, especially working-class men and women. "I cannot paint an angel," said the French realist Gustave Courbet (koor BAY) "because I have never seen one." Instead, he painted works such as *The Stone Breakers,* which shows two rough laborers on a country road. Later in the century, *The Gross Clinic,* by American painter Thomas Eakins, shocked viewers with its realistic depiction of an autopsy conducted in a medical classroom.

Vocabulary Builder
emphasis—(EM fuh sis) *n.* special attention given to something to make it stand out

✓ **Checkpoint** How did the realism movement differ from the romantic movement?

Chapter 9 Section 4 321

The Visual Arts Take New Directions

By the 1840s, a new art form, photography, was emerging. **Louis Daguerre** (dah GEHR) in France and William Fox Talbot in England had improved on earlier technologies to produce successful photographs. At first, many photos were stiff, posed portraits of middle-class families or prominent people. Other photographs reflected the romantics' fascination with faraway places.

In time, photographers used the camera to present the grim realities of life. During the American Civil War, Mathew B. Brady preserved a vivid, realistic record of the corpse-strewn battlefields. Other photographers showed the harsh conditions in industrial factories or slums.

The Impressionists Photography posed a challenge to painters. Why try for realism, some artists asked, when a camera could do the same thing better? By the 1870s, a group of painters took art in a new direction, seeking to capture the first fleeting impression made by a scene or object on the viewer's eye. The new movement, known as **impressionism**, took root in Paris, capital of the Western art world.

Since the Renaissance, painters had carefully finished their paintings so that no brush strokes showed. But impressionists like **Claude Monet** (moh NAY) and Edgar Degas (day GAH) brushed strokes of color side by side without any blending. According to new scientific studies of optics, the human eye would mix these patches of color.

By concentrating on visual impressions rather than realism, artists achieved a fresh view of familiar subjects. Monet, for example, painted the cathedral at Rouen (roo AHN), France, dozens of times from the same angle, capturing how it looked in different lights at different times of day.

The Postimpressionists Later painters, called postimpressionists, developed a variety of styles. Georges Seurat (suh RAH) arranged small dots of color to define the shapes of objects. **Vincent van Gogh** experimented with sharp brush lines and bright colors. His unique brushwork lent a dreamlike quality to everyday subjects. Paul Gauguin (goh GAN) also developed a bold, personal style. In his paintings, people look flat, as in "primitive" folk art. But his brooding colors and black outlining of shapes convey intense feelings and images.

✓ **Checkpoint** How did photography influence the development of painting?

Postimpressionism
This self-portrait of Dutch painter Vincent van Gogh shows his bandaged ear, which he cut off in a state of depression. *What postimpressionist features are demonstrated in Van Gogh's self-portrait?*

Vocabulary Builder
intense—(in TENS) *adj.* very strong or deep

Section 4 Assessment

Progress Monitoring Online
For: Self-quiz with vocabulary practice
Web Code: nba-2141

Terms, People, and Places
1. For each term, person, or place listed at the beginning of the section, write a sentence explaining its significance.

Note Taking
2. **Reading Skill: Identify Supporting Details** Use your completed table to answer the Focus Question: What artistic movements emerged in reaction to the Industrial Revolution?

Comprehension and Critical Thinking
3. **Summarize** What are three subjects romantics favored?
4. **Draw Conclusions** What did Courbet mean when he said, "I cannot paint an angel because I have never seen one"? Do you agree with his attitude? Explain.
5. **Recognize Cause and Effect** In what ways were the new artistic styles of the 1800s a reaction to changes in society?

● **Writing About History**
Quick Write: Support a Solution Based on what you've read, list supporting information, such as details, data, and facts, for the following thesis statement of a problem-solution essay: Artists in the 1800s portrayed subjects realistically to make the public more aware of some of the grim problems of life in industrialized nations.

322 Life in the Industrial Age

Unit 3: Reading and Taking Notes from Textbooks

Activity 3-6: Practice Using PQRW (continued)

Now, complete the question, read, and write steps of PQRW for Section 4.

Title of Textbook: _____

Title of Chapter: _____

Title of Chapter Part: _____

Heading: _____

Question: _____

Answer: _____

_____

_____

Heading: _____

Question: _____

Answer: _____

_____

_____

Heading: _____

Question: _____

Answer: _____

_____

_____

Unit 3: Reading and Taking Notes from Textbooks

Activity 3-6: Practice Using PQRW (continued)

Heading: _____
Question: _____
Answer: _____
_____
_____
_____

Heading: _____
Question: _____
Answer: _____
_____
_____
_____

Heading: _____
Question: _____
Answer: _____
_____
_____
_____

Heading: _____
Question: _____
Answer: _____
_____
_____
_____

Unit 3: Reading and Taking Notes from Textbooks

Activity 3-6: Practice Using PQRW (continued)

Heading: _____
Question: _____
Answer: _____
_____
_____

Heading: _____
Question: _____
Answer: _____
_____
_____

Heading: _____
Question: _____
Answer: _____
_____
_____

Heading: _____
Question: _____
Answer: _____
_____
_____

Unit 3: Reading and Taking Notes from Textbooks

Activity 3-6: Practice Using PQRW (continued)

Heading: _____

Question: _____

Answer: _____

_____

_____

_____

Heading: _____

Question: _____

Answer: _____

_____

_____

_____

Heading: _____

Question: _____

Answer: _____

_____

_____

_____

Heading: _____

Question: _____

Answer: _____

_____

_____

_____

Unit 3: Reading and Taking Notes from Textbooks

Activity 3-6: Practice Using PQRW (continued)

Heading: _____
Question: _____
Answer: _____
_____
_____

Heading: _____
Question: _____
Answer: _____
_____
_____

Heading: _____
Question: _____
Answer: _____
_____
_____

Heading: _____
Question: _____
Answer: _____
_____
_____

Activity 3-7: What I Have Learned

Use the PQRW strategy with a chapter from a textbook that you are using in school. Write labels as needed.

Unit 3: Reading and Taking Notes from Textbooks
Activity 3-7: What I Have Learned (continued)

Unit 3: Reading and Taking Notes from Textbooks

Activity 3-7: What I Have Learned (continued)

Unit 4
Taking Notes in Class

Activities

4-1   Identifying Signal Words and Statements

4-2   Using the Fewest Words

4-3   Using Common Abbreviations for Words

4-4   Using Your Own Abbreviations for Words

4-5   Using Abbreviations for Terms

4-6   Using Symbols for Words or Terms

4-7   A Two-Column Notetaking Format

4-8   Taking First Notes

4-9   Rewriting First Notes

4-10 Creating a Graphic Organizer for Rewritten Notes

4-11 Recognizing Other Lecture Styles

4-12 What I Have Learned

Activity 4-1: Identifying Signal Words and Statements

As your teachers lecture in class, they will often use words and statements to alert you that what they are about to say is important to write in your notes. These words and statements are called **signal words and statements**.

1. **Here are some signal words and statements that teachers frequently use. Place a check next to any that you have heard your teachers use.**

    The most important point…

    Next…

    Write in your notes…

    Be sure to remember…

    Keep in mind…

    Therefore…

    It is significant…

    In conclusion…

    The major thing to know…

    Similarly…

    Be sure you understand…

    Moveover…

    Make sure you know…

    Finally…

    As a result…

    I am going to expect you to…

    Listen carefully as I…

    However…

    It should be noted…

    A central issue…

    This will be on the test…

Unit 4: Taking Notes in Class

Activity 4-1: Identifying Signal Words and Statements (continued)

2. **Read the following class lecture about blood circulation. Underline each signal word and signal statement each time it occurs.**

> Today we are going to talk about how blood circulates through the human body. Probably the most important point to keep in mind is that the heart plays an important role in this process. When the heart contracts it pushes the blood out into two major loops or cycles. When thinking about how blood circulates, remember that there are two cycles. One cycle is the systemic cycle. In this cycle the blood circulates into the body systems. Consequently, oxygen is supplied to the body's organs, structures, and tissues. Furthermore, carbon dioxide waste is collected. The second cycle is the pulmonary cycle. In this cycle, the blood circulates to and from the lungs. As a result, carbon dioxide is released and new oxygen is picked up. It is significant that the systemic cycle is controlled by the left side of the heart, while the pulmonary cycle is controlled by the right side. Keep in mind that although the circulatory system is made up of two cycles, both happen at the same time. It is estimated that it takes about 30 seconds for a portion of blood to complete the entire cycle.
>
> Before we stop I want to mention the aorta. This is one of the terms that will be on the test next week. It is the largest artery of the body and is an inch wide. Also, make sure you know about the superior vena cava and the inferior vena cava. They are the two largest veins. Finally, what do you think a normal heart rate is at rest? It's about 72 beats per minute.

3. **Think of some other signal words and signal statements you have heard your teachers use. Write them here.**

_____

_____

_____

_____

_____

_____

Unit 4: Taking Notes in Class

Activity 4-2: Using the Fewest Words

Activity 4-2: Using the Fewest Words

Teachers in high school usually talk at a rate of about 100 to 120 words per minute. The average high school student can write about 15 to 20 words per minute. Because teachers talk more quickly than you can write, it is important to write your notes as quickly as possible to capture the important information.

One way to increase your notetaking speed is to write the fewest words needed. You can do this by writing short sentences or phrases in place of long sentences.

Look at this information provided by a teacher during an oral presentation:

Leaves help all kinds of plants to draw water up from the soil by a process that scientists call transpiration.

Now look at the shortened version of this information that follows. Notice that although there are fewer words, none of the important information has been lost.

Leaves help plants draw water from soil by transpiration.

For each of the following, rewrite the information using the fewest words needed without losing any of the important information.

1. Romanticism does not refer to romance in the sense of an affectionate relationship but rather to an artistic style emphasizing imagination, freedom, and emotion.

2. The Liberal party passed some social legislation, but it traditionally represented middle-class business interests.

3. It must be stressed that only certain cells, called target cells, can respond to certain hormones.

4. Spurred on by the support of Luther, nobles suppressed the Peasants' Revolt, killing tens of thousands of people and leaving thousands more homeless.

5. If the bones are thin, it is worthwhile to take all possible measures to gain bone density because even a slight increase can significantly reduce the risk of one or more bones fracturing.

Activity 4-3: Using Common Abbreviations for Words

Another way to increase your notetaking speed is to use **abbreviations**. An abbreviation is a shortened form of a word that is used in place of the whole word. Many words have commonly used abbreviations. For example, *psych* is often used as an abbreviation for *psychology*. Sometimes the same abbreviation is used for more than one word. For example, *vet* is used as an abbreviation for *veteran* and *veterinarian*. For abbreviations that apply to more than one word, the context of your notes will tell you what the whole word is. If the lecture was about the problems faced by veterans returning from a war, *vet* would obviously be an abbreviation for *veteran*. If the lecture had been about medical fields of study, *vet* would obviously be an abbreviation for *veterinarian*.

There are some rules that require an abbreviation to be followed by a period. Since the concern here is to increase notetaking speed, do not worry about these rules. Simply write all abbreviations without periods.

Here are some commonly used abbreviations for words. Write the whole word for each abbreviation.

1. bldg _____
2. ht _____
3. mgr _____
4. geom _____
5. jr _____
6. misc _____
7. sch _____
8. blvd _____
9. ave _____
10. sec _____
11. div _____
12. govt _____
13. pct _____
14. inc _____

Activity 4-4: Using Your Own Abbreviations for Words

You can form your own abbreviations for words that do not have common abbreviations or whose common abbreviations you do not know.

It is very important that when you form your own abbreviation for a word, you will be able to identify the whole word when you look back at your notes. When you are not sure what word your abbreviation represents, the context of the lecture and your set of notes will help you to identify the word. Do not overdo your use of abbreviations. Too many abbreviations will make it difficult for you to read and review your notes.

Here are three ways you can form your own abbreviations for words.

For words whose beginning is easy to pronounce, write just the beginning of the word. For example, you can write the abbreviation *recip* for *reciprocal*, or *kin* for *kinetic*.

For words that do not begin with a vowel, omit the vowel or vowels. For example, *fcts* for *facetious*, or *lxcn* for *lexicon*.

For words that have just one syllable, write just the first and last letter. For example *qk* for *quark*, or *ge* for *gauche*.

Write an abbreviation for each of the following words. For each word, use the way of forming abbreviations that you think works best for the word.

1. bibliography _____
2. paradigm _____
3. auspicious _____
4. auditorium _____
5. strait _____
6. mitosis _____
7. lane _____
8. institute _____
9. telephone _____
10. lecture _____
11. plateau _____
12. industry _____
13. prime _____
14. hydroelectricity _____
15. root _____
16. sensible _____

Activity 4-5: Using Abbreviations for Terms

Terms are groups of words that have a particular meaning. Like words, terms can be abbreviated.

Many terms are the names of organizations or entities. Many other terms are expressions used in everyday language. Terms that are commonly used are often abbreviated by writing only the first letter of each word in the term. For example, *CIA* is a commonly used abbreviation for *Central Intelligence Agency*. The first letter of a small word in a term (e.g., *and, or, of*) is usually omitted from the abbreviation. For example, *eta* is the commonly used abbreviation for the term *estimated time of arrival*. Notice that "of" was not included in the abbreviation.

Here are some abbreviations for commonly used terms. For each abbreviation, write the full term next to its abbreviation.

1. faq _____
2. EST _____
3. awd _____
4. NFL _____
5. obo _____
6. mpg _____
7. asap _____
8. FBI _____
9. USPS _____
10. sro _____
11. AWOL _____
12. M.D. _____
13. rpm _____
14. e.g. _____

Activity 4-6: Using Symbols for Words or Terms

Another way to write notes quickly is to use **symbols** for words or terms, and to write numerals instead of number words (e.g., 7 for seven). Here are some words and terms and their commonly used symbols.

Σ	sum	&	and	Ψ	psychology
@	at	#	number	$	dollar
=	equals, equal to	?	question	c/o	care of
™	trademark	√	check	Δ	increment
÷	divided by	≠	not equal to	\	difference
>	greater than	<	less than	%	percentage
∞	infinity	≈	almost equal to	±	plus or minus
'	minute	€	euro	©	copyright

Rewrite each of the following sentences using what you have learned about writing the fewest words and using abbreviations and symbols.

1. Ellen wanted the United States Postal Service to deliver the package as soon as possible to her neighbor's house care of Mister Williams.

   _____

   _____

2. The attorney tried to use the psychology he had learned in college thirty years ago when he argued his latest case that afternoon about a trademark before the United States Circuit Court.

   _____

   _____

3. Leslie was interested in attending the Federal Bureau of Investigation conference to be held on the eighteenth at a building on a university campus that the organizers expected to draw a standing-room-only audience of more than three hundred, plus or minus a few attendees.

   _____

   _____

Unit 4: Taking Notes in Class

Activity 4-7: A Two-Column Notetaking Format

Activity 4-7: A Two-Column Notetaking Format

Your teachers may use a variety of lecture styles. The lecture style used most frequently by teachers is the main ideas-supporting details style. When using this style, the teacher will begin by identifying the topic. The topic is what the lecture is about. As the lecture proceeds, the teacher will present a number of main ideas about the topic. A main idea is a major idea about the topic. Number words such as *one* or *first*, and transitional words such as *next, another, then,* and *finally,* are used to delineate the main ideas. The teacher will also provide supporting details about each of the main ideas. A supporting detail provides specific information about a main idea.

Use the *two-column notetaking format* shown below when your teacher uses the main ideas-supporting details lecture style.

Class _____   Date _____

Page Number _____   Topic _____

Main Ideas	Supporting Details

133

Copyright Mangrum-Strichart Learning Resources
www.mangrum-strichart.com

Unit 4: Taking Notes in Class

Activity 4-7: A Two-Column Notetaking Format (continued)

Here is how to take notes during class using the two-column notetaking format. The notes you take in class are your first notes. Remember to listen for signal words and statements to be sure you include all of the important information. Use abbreviated words, symbols, and shortened sentences or phrases to write your notes quickly.

1. Record the name of the class you are taking notes for, the date of the class session, and the page number of the notes for that class session. Many times you will have more than one page of notes for the session.

2. Write the topic of the lecture once your teacher identifies it.

3. Each time your teacher provides a main idea, write it in the Main Ideas column. Number each main idea beginning with 1.

4. Next to each main idea, write in the Supporting Details column any supporting details your teacher provides about the main idea. Number each supporting detail for a main idea beginning with 1.

5. Place a question mark at the end of any main idea or supporting detail that you write but do not fully understand.

6. Underline any word used by your teacher that you write but whose meaning you are not sure about.

Answer these questions.

1. What is a topic?

   _____

2. What is a main idea?

   _____

3. What is a supporting detail?

   _____

4. What should you do to write notes quickly?

   _____

Unit 4: Taking Notes in Class

Activity 4-7: A Two-Column Notetaking Format (continued)

5. What should you do if you do not fully understand a main idea or a supporting detail that you write in your notes?

   _____

6. What should you do when you write a word in your notes whose meaning you are not sure about?

   _____

7. Why should you write the page number on your notes?

   _____

8. What are two types of words that teachers use to delineate main ideas?

   _____

9. What are the notes you take in class called?

   _____

10. What can help you to identify information that you should definitely write in your notes?

    _____

Unit 4: Taking Notes in Class

Activity 4-8: Taking First Notes

Activity 4-8: Taking First Notes

The written notes you take in class are **first notes**. You will learn how to rewrite your first notes in Activity 4-9.

Because you need to write your notes quickly while in class, your first notes should consist of short sentences and phrases, along with the use of abbreviations and symbols where appropriate. There may be question marks at the ends of some main ideas and supporting details, and some unknown words that are underlined. Do not worry about punctuation and spelling when taking first notes. You will provide punctuation and correct any spelling errors when you rewrite your notes.

Read the following lecture presented by a teacher in a social studies class. The teacher used the main ideas-supporting details lecture style.

> If everyone is ready, we'll get started. Today I want to talk about why we put people in prison. There are almost two million people in America's jails at the local, state, and federal levels. And the number is growing. I saw an interesting statistic that America has five percent of the world's population but twenty five percent of the number of people incarcerated in the world. It is important to know that there are four main reasons why we place people in prison. The first reason is retribution. This is a pretty easy reason to understand. Basically we put people in prison to punish them for something they did wrong. Keep in mind that some people regard this as a way to have people who commit a crime repay their debt to society. Deterrence is another reason for putting people in prison. It is thought that if people know they will have to go to prison for committing a crime, they will be less likely to commit a crime. Be sure to remember that some experts maintain that prison sentences must be sufficiently long to serve as a powerful deterrent. The next reason for putting people in prison is to try to rehabilitate them. It is significant that more and more of society hopes that we can change the behavior of people who commit crimes so they become conforming members of society. Moreover, another goal of the rehabilitation model of imprisonment is to provide inmates with education and training so they will have the skills to support themselves without resorting to crime. Finally, there is incapacitation. As long as a prisoner is in jail, he or she can't be out on the street committing crimes or hurting people. We'll talk more about these reasons tomorrow.

On the next page, examine the first notes a student took in class from the lecture about why we put people in prison.

Unit 4: Taking Notes in Class

Activity 4-8: Taking First Notes (continued)

Class _____ Social Studies _____   Date _____ 11/10 _____
Page Number _____ 1 _____   Topic _____ Why we put people in prison _____

Main Ideas	Supporting Details
1. put ppl in pris 4 <u>retrebution</u>	1. punish 2. pay dbt 2 soc?
2. 4 <u>deterrence</u>	1. so ppl no they go 2 pris 2. make sent lng
3. rehab them	1. chng behav 2. educ & trng 3. prvd skls so don't need 2 commit crms
4. <u>incapacitation</u>	1. keep off st

Unit 4: Taking Notes in Class

Activity 4-8: Taking First Notes (continued)

Use the first notes to answer the following questions.

1. What was the lecture about?
   _____

2. How many main ideas were there?
   _____

3. Write each word whose meaning the student was unsure about.
   _____

4. Which main idea had the most supporting details?
   _____

5. What idea will the student need to clarify?
   _____

6. What symbols did the student use?
   _____

7. Was at least one supporting detail provided for each main idea?
   _____

8. Use the context of the lecture to write the whole word for the following abbreviations used by the student.

   st _____

   chng_____

   soc _____

9. Write the correct spellings of any words the student may have misspelled.

   _____

   _____

   _____

Unit 4: Taking Notes in Class

Activity 4-9: Rewriting First Notes

Activity 4-9: Rewriting First Notes

As soon as possible after class, rewrite your first notes. Your rewritten notes should be complete and accurate.

Rewriting your notes can be helpful to you in several ways.

- You will have an opportunity to correct any errors you might have in your first notes.
- As you rewrite your notes, you will be reviewing what you wrote. This will help you to remember the information in your notes.
- You will be left with a clear set of notes that will make it easier for you to study for a test.

Here is what to do when you rewrite your first notes.

- Replace each abbreviation with the whole word.
- Replace each symbol with the word the symbol represents.
- Expand short sentences and phrases into full sentences with punctuation.
- Correct any spelling errors.
- If you placed a question at the end of a main idea or supporting detail, use your textbooks and reference sources to clarify the idea or detail. Incorporate what you learn about the main idea or supporting detail.
- If you underlined a word, use a print or online dictionary to learn the meaning of the word. Incorporate what you learn about the meaning of the word.

Unit 4: Taking Notes in Class

Activity 4-9: Rewriting First Notes (continued)

Use the two-column notetaking form below to rewrite the first notes shown in Activity 4-8.

Class _____   Date _____

Page Number _____   Topic _____

Main Ideas	Supporting Details

Unit 4: Taking Notes in Class

Activity 4-10: Creating a Graphic Organizer for Rewritten Notes

Activity 4-10: Creating a Graphic Organizer for Rewritten Notes

Once you have rewritten your notes, create a **graphic organizer** for your rewritten notes. A graphic organizer provides a visual picture of information that allows you to easily see the relationships between facts, terms, and ideas. It is an excellent tool when you want to quickly review your notes.

When a teacher uses the main ideas-supporting details lecture style, a graphic organizer for rewritten notes consists of a center oval for the topic of the lecture, connecting ovals for each main idea, and connecting lines for each supporting detail. Write above and below a supporting detail line if needed. Do not write anything on the lines that connect the main ideas to the center (topic) oval.

Complete the blank graphic organizer form provided below for your rewritten notes from Activity 4-9. You may not need to use all of the ovals and lines provided.

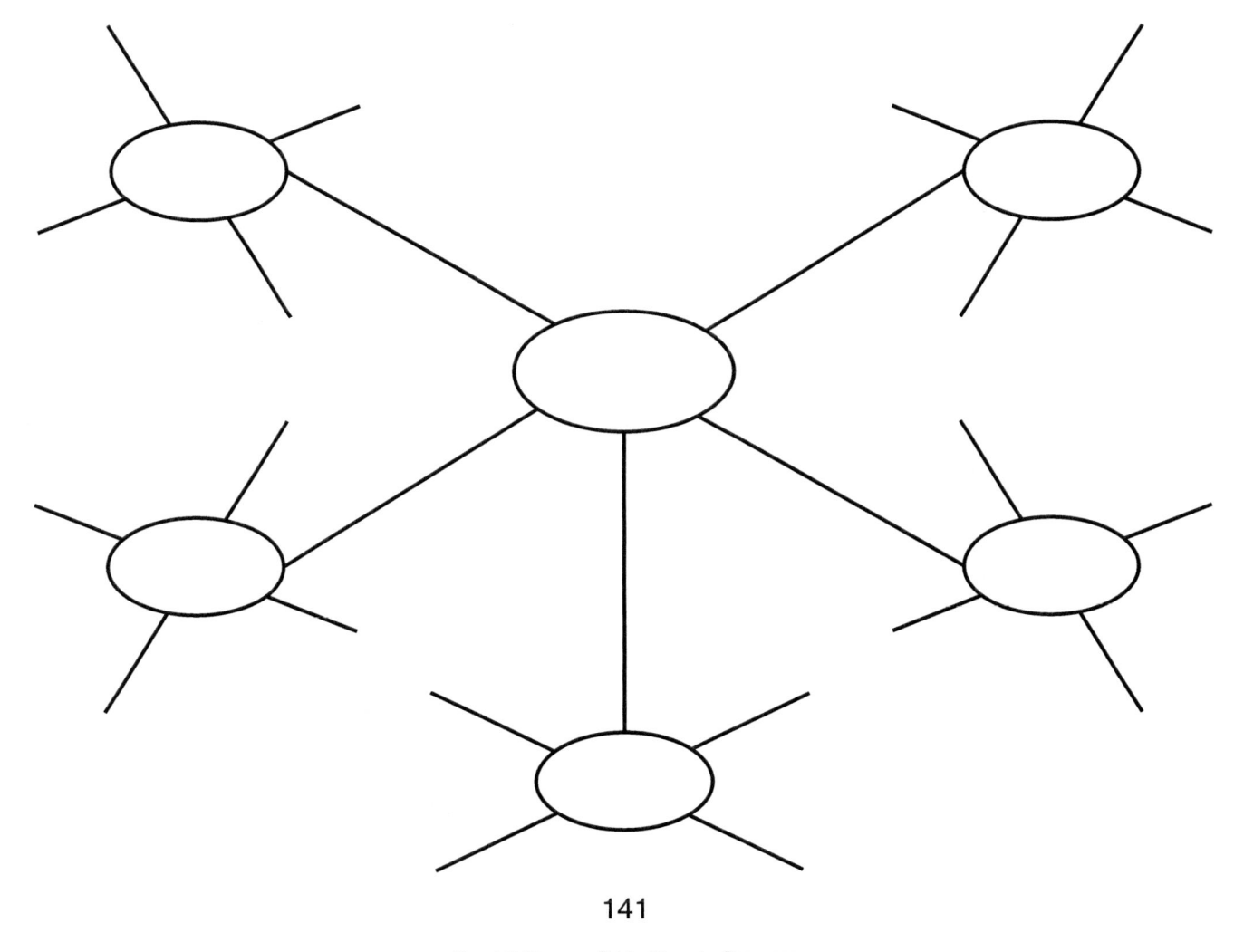

Unit 4: Taking Notes in Class

Activity 4-11: Recognizing Other Lecture Styles

Activity 4-11: Recognizing Other Lecture Styles

As you learned in Activity 4-7, the main ideas-supporting details lecture style is the style used most frequently by teachers. In this activity you will learn about five other lecture styles that teachers sometimes use. Becoming familiar with these styles will help you to take better written notes in class.

The two-column notetaking format you learned about in Activity 4-7 can be used with these other lecture styles by simply changing the Main Ideas and Supporting Details headings. You will be able to create appropriate graphic organizers for your rewritten notes for the other lecture styles by using the information taught in Unit 7.

Question-Answer Lecture Style—In this style, the teacher introduces a topic followed by one or more questions. Each question is answered after it is introduced. Details are included with an answer as needed. Words and phrases such as *who, what, where, when, why, how, and in what way(s)* indicate that a question-answer lecture style is being used. Use Questions, and Answers, as the headings for the two-column notetaking format. Activity 7-2 shows how to create a question-answer graphic organizer.

Read the following lecture that a teacher presented in a question-answer style.

> Think about an element such as gold being cut into pieces that are smaller and smaller. At a certain point the pieces become too small to be seen even with a microscope. Now just imagine you keep doing this cutting until you end up with the smallest piece of matter that still has the chemical properties of gold. What do you call this smallest piece of matter? It is called an atom. An atom is defined as the smallest part of an element that has the chemical properties of that element. All matter is made of atoms. Who do you think first thought about atoms? It wasn't Einstein. It was long before his time. It was the ancient Greeks who first hypothesized about atoms. It wasn't until the early 1800's that scientists began to get a good understanding of atoms. Does anyone here know the name of the scientist who developed an atomic theory of matter that helped to explain what atoms were? He was English. His name was John Dalton, and his theory motivated other scientists to learn more about atoms.

Unit 4: Taking Notes in Class

Activity 4-11: Recognizing Other Lecture Styles (continued)

Answer these questions about the lecture.

1. What is the topic?

   _____

2. What words and/or phrases indicated that a question-answer lecture style was used?

   _____

3. What three questions did the teacher ask during the lecture?

   _____

Compare-Contrast Lecture Style—When using the compare-contrast lecture style, the teacher begins by identifying two things that will be compared and contrasted. The teacher then describes how the two things are similar and how they are different. Certain words and phrases indicate that a compare-contrast style is being used. For example, *compare, alike, similarly, correspondingly, in parallel, counterpart, equal to, resemble,* and *just as* suggest similarities. Words or phrases such as *differently, in contrast, however, difference between, antithesis of, disparity, distinction, in comparison, on the other hand, opposite,* and *on the contrary* suggest differences. Use Similarities, and Differences, as the headings for the two-column notetaking format. Activity 7-3 shows how to create a compare-contrast graphic organizer.

Read the following lecture that a teacher presented in a compare-contrast style.

Let's compare and contrast high school and college. Here we are near the end of the school year. Many of you are close to finishing high school and are thinking about going to college. In high school, classes meet every day. College classes usually meet only two or three times a week. Here in high school you find the same students in most of your classes. On the other hand, in college you will find many different students in your classes. Just like in high school, you will get assignments on the first day of class. Unlike in high school, though, your college teachers will not keep reminding you about your assignments later on. High school and college are similar in that you have to study hard in both places. But in contrast to high school, where you can depend on teachers to monitor your work, you will need to be much more independent in college.

Unit 4: Taking Notes in Class

Activity 4-11: Recognizing Other Lecture Styles (continued)

Answer these questions about the lecture.

4. What words and/or phrases in the presentation indicated that a compare-contrast style was used?

   _____

5. What two things are being compared and contrasted?

   _____

6. What are two similarities between them?

   _____

7. What are two differences between them?

   _____

Series of Events Lecture Style—When using the series of events lecture style, the teacher begins by identifying the topic. Then the teacher presents information about an initial event, step, or stage related to the topic followed by information about additional events, steps, or stages. The presentation is concluded when the teacher describes the final event, step, or stage. Words or phrases such as *first, initially, at the outset, second, next, followed by, then, later, after, succeeding, intermediate, last, culminating,* and *finally* indicate that a series of events lecture style is being used. Use Events, and Supporting Details, as the headings for the two-column notetaking format. Activity 7-4 shows how to create a series of events graphic organizer.

On the following page, read the lecture that a teacher presented in a series of events style.

Unit 4: Taking Notes in Class

Activity 4-11: Recognizing Other Lecture Styles (continued)

> Butterflies develop from eggs through a process called metamorphosis. Copy that word from the chalkboard into your notes. Metamorphosis is a Greek word that means a change in shape. Butterflies actually develop in four stages. The first stage is the Egg stage. Adult female butterflies lay eggs on plants. This is followed by the second stage in which the caterpillars hatch from the eggs. This stage is called the Larva stage. The hatching usually occurs during the summer. The caterpillars eat the plants on which the eggs were laid in the first stage. Here is something incredible for you to know. During the Larva stage caterpillars grow a hundred times their size and reach a length of two inches over a few weeks. The Pupa stage is the next stage of development. Just like bears, caterpillars stop eating and hibernate. They transform themselves into a pupa and remain inside a cocoon that protects them. The culminating stage is the Adult stage. At this point the butterfly as we know it emerges and flies about pollinating plants and reproducing.

Answer these questions about the lecture.

8. What is the topic?

   _____

9. What words and/or phrases indicated a series of events lecture style was used?

   _____

10. What are the four stages in the development of a butterfly?

    _____

Unit 4: Taking Notes in Class

Activity 4-11: Recognizing Other Lecture Styles (continued)

Cause–Effect Lecture Style—When the cause-effect lecture style is used, the teacher begins by presenting the cause of something, followed by one or more effects that are related to the cause. Words or phrases like *since, thus, therefore, because, consequently, accordingly, so, hence, for that reason, inasmuch as, on account of, owing to, due to, whereas,* and *as a result* indicate that a cause-effect lecture style is being used. Use Cause, and Effects, as the headings for the two-column notetaking format. Activity 7-5 shows how to create a cause-effect graphic organizer.

Read the following lecture that a teacher presented in a cause-effect style.

> Deaths and injuries in automobile accidents are of great concern to the automobile industry. Thus the industry is taking steps to reduce these. Owing to the high incidence of deaths and injuries from front-end impact in automobile accidents, manufacturers are installing both driver and passenger front air bags in their vehicles. As a result of their concern, some manufacturers are even placing side air bags to provide protection from side-impact automobile accidents. Does your family car have side air bags? In any event, engines are now mounted so that upon impact they move downward rather than into the passenger compartment. Manufacturers are also strengthening automobile frames to better withstand impacts. They are doing so by placing extra metal supports in the door frames. Beyond these structural changes, manufacturers have sponsored consumer education programs to promote safe driving habits. Some of these programs are directed toward adults, while others are designed for teenage drivers. Consequently, we have a driver education class in our school.

Answer these questions about the lecture.

11. What is the lecture about?

12. What words and/or phrases indicated that a cause-effect lecture style was being used?

13. What cause is presented?

14. Identify three effects related to this cause.

Unit 4: Taking Notes in Class

Activity 4-11: Recognizing Other Lecture Styles (continued)

Problem-Solution Lecture Style—When this lecture style is used, the teacher begins by introducing a problem and explaining why it is a problem. The teacher continues by describing attempts to solve the problem, providing details as necessary. The teacher concludes by identifying the solution to the problem or the status of attempts to solve the problem.

The following words or phrases indicate that a problem-solution style is being used. Words or phrases like *problem, point of dispute, subject of dispute, puzzle, conundrum, enigma, issue, bafflement, tough nut to crack*, and *complication* indicate that a problem is being presented. Words or phrases like *solution, solve, answer, attempt, explanation, explication, recommend, interpretation, resolve, elucidate, clear up, unravel, work out,* and *untangle* indicate that a solution has been achieved or is underway. Use Problem, and Attempted Solutions, as the headings for the two-column notetaking format. Activity 7-6 shows how to create a problem-solution graphic organizer.

Read the following lecture that a teacher presented in a problem-solution style.

> Coronary heart disease is an issue throughout the world. This dreaded disease is killing many people. A friend of mine died of this disease two years ago. To try to solve this problem, doctors recommend that we eat less meat. Meat contains too much fat and cholesterol. Another explanation for the high incidence of heart disease is smoking. Many doctors recommend that people stop using tobacco products. Smoking constricts blood vessels and therefore raises blood pressure. Another answer to the problem may be for people to add more activity to their lifestyle. Reducing weight to ideal body weight reduces the risk of heart disease. Until people implement these recommendations, coronary heart disease will remain a problem throughout the world.

Unit 4: Taking Notes in Class

Activity 4-11: Recognizing Other Lecture Styles (continued)

Answer these questions about the lecture.

15. What is the problem?

   _____

16. What words and/or phrases indicated a problem-solution lecture style was used?

   _____

17. What words and/or phrases indicated a solution or an attempt at a solution?

   _____

18. Identify two attempts to solve the problem.

   _____

19. Has the problem been solved?

   _____

Activity 4-12: What I Have Learned

Answer the following.

1. What are three ways to write notes quickly?

   _____
   _____
   _____

2. What are three ways to form abbreviations?

   _____
   _____
   _____

3. Why do teachers use signal words and statements when they lecture?

   _____

4. Identify three signal words or statements often used by teachers.

   _____
   _____
   _____

5. What is a main idea?

   _____

6. When writing first notes, what should you do when you write a word in your notes whose meaning you are not sure about?

   _____

7. When rewriting your first notes, what should you do for any symbols you used?

   _____

8. What are two benefits of creating a graphic organizer for your rewritten notes?

   _____

Unit 4: Taking Notes in Class

Activity 4-12: What I Have Learned (continued)

9. Which lecture style does the word *what* indicate?

10. Which lecture style does the word *explanation* indicate?

11. Which lecture style does the phrase *on the other hand* indicate?

12. Which lecture style does the word *succeeding* indicate?

13. Which lecture style does the word *hence* indicate?

14. What is a topic?

15. Why do you think it is important to include the date when you take notes in class?

Unit 5
Using Reference Sources

Activities

5-1   The Internet

5-2   Dictionary

5-3   Choosing the Correct Meaning

5-4   Thesaurus

5-5   Practice Using a Thesaurus

5-6   Choosing the Correct Synonym

5-7   Encyclopedia

5-8   Almanac

5-9   Statistical Abstract of the United States

5-10 Atlas

5-11 Occupational Outlook Handbook

5-12 What I Have Learned

Activity 5-1: The Internet

The Internet is a major means of finding information about any topic. When using the Internet to find information, keep in mind that the information on the Internet is largely unfiltered. That is, anyone can create a website and put information on it without the information being reviewed and verified by appropriate experts. It is very possible that a website is simply someone's opinion, may be based on a misconception, and might be inaccurate. It is therefore important that you evaluate a website and the information it provides before using the information.

Here are five criteria to use to evaluate information found at a website. You should only use information from a website if all of these criteria are met.

1. **Authority.** Look to see if the author of the information is identified. Be cautious if the author is not identified. Sometimes the author is an agency or organization. If the author is identified, look for indications that the author is qualified to write about the topic.

2. **Accuracy.** Try to determine if the information provided is reliable and free from errors. Look to see if the author drew upon high quality sources of information. Also, compare the information with other websites that provide similar information. If the author seems to be trying to sell something, go to another website.

3. **Objectivity.** Be cautious if you sense that the author appears to be biased in some way. Look for websites that have information that is balanced and with no indication of a conflict of interest.

4. **Currency.** Look to see when the information was put up. One of the great advantages of the Internet is that you can find information that is right up to date. Information changes rapidly, so avoid information that is not current.

5. **Coverage.** Look for information that is in-depth and organized. A website can be particularly valuable if it provides information that is difficult to find elsewhere.

Identify a topic. Then locate a website that provides information about that topic. Complete the form on the following page once you have done this. For each of the five criteria, write whether the criterion has been met, and why or why not.

Unit 5: Using Reference Sources

Activity 5-1: The Internet (continued)

Topic	
Name of Website	
Authority	
Accuracy	
Objectivity	
Currency	
Coverage	

Activity 5-2: Dictionary

As is the case for all of the reference sources presented in this unit, dictionaries are available in both print and online editions. As the use of the Internet becomes increasingly widespread, you will find fewer print options and more online options. However, the information provided by various reference sources remains similar whether in print or online.

A **dictionary** is a reference book that focuses on defining words. Dictionaries include most or all of the frequently used words in a language. Each word that is listed and defined in a dictionary is referred to as an entry word.

You will find the following types of information about entry words in a dictionary.

Definitions. One or more meanings of an entry word are presented for each part of speech in which the word is used. For example, the word *buckle* is used as both a noun and a verb. Because *buckle* is more frequently used as a noun than as a verb, meanings for its use as a noun are presented first in order of their frequency of use. Meanings are then provided in order of their frequency of use for *buckle* when used as a verb. For many words, there is just one part of speech. For example, *hyperbole* is used only as a noun.

The parts of speech for entry words are typically abbreviated as follows:

n. = noun   *pron. = pronoun*

v. = verb   *adv. = adverb*

adj. = adjective   *prep. = preposition*

con. = conjunction

Syllabication. The entry word is shown broken into syllables. The entry word *buckle* is shown as buck-le.

Phonetic respelling. A phonetic respelling of the entry word to show you how to pronounce it. The phonetic respelling uses letters and symbols to show you how to pronounce the word. A pronunciation key is provided for the letters and symbols used. The phonetic respelling of the entry word *buckle* may be shown as [**buhk**-uhl]. If you are using an online dictionary, you can also hear the word pronounced correctly.

Origin or etymology. Information is provided about the history of the entry word from one language to another as far back as can be determined with reasonable certainty. For example, for the entry word *buckle*, the information presented might be that the word is derived from the Middle English word *bocle (1300-50)*, which meant the cheekpiece of a helmet.

Unit 5: Using Reference Sources
Activity 5-2: Dictionary (continued)

Depending on the dictionary you use, you may find some or all of the following types of information.

Synonyms. A synonym is a word that has the same or nearly the same meaning as another word. For example, one definition of the entry word *buckle* might be to bend, warp, bulge, or collapse. A synonym such as *sag* or *crumple* might be provided for this meaning of *buckle*.

Antonyms. An antonym is a word that has the opposite or nearly the opposite meaning of another word. For example, for the definition of *buckle* as to bend, warp, bulge, or collapse, antonyms such as *flatten* or *smooth* might be provided.

Use in a sentence. For example, for the meaning of the entry word *buckle* as a clasp for fastening together two loose ends on a belt or strap, you might find the following sentence: Because he had lost some weight, he tightened the buckle of his belt to help keep his pants up.

Use in a phrase. The meanings of phrases using the entry word may be shown. For example, for the entry word *buckle*, the meanings of *buckle down* (to set to work with vigor) and *buckle up* (to fasten one's seat belt) might be provided.

Dictionaries, especially online dictionaries, continue to add more types of information about words. You may find quotations that use the word, idioms that use the word, the use of the word as slang, as well as related words.

Locate the entry word *transport* in a dictionary. Then, complete the form on the following page for the information found in the dictionary about *transport*. Write only the information that is in the dictionary. Do not write your own sentences, synonyms, etc. Write "None" for any type of information the dictionary did not provide.

Unit 5: Using Reference Sources

Activity 5-2: Dictionary (continued)

Name of Dictionary	
Most Frequently Used Meaning for Each Part of Speech in Which the Word is Used. Specify the part of speech the meaning applies to.	
Syllabication	
Phonetic Respelling	
Origin or Etymology	
Synonyms	
Antonyms	
Use in a Sentence	
Use in a Phrase	
Other Information	

Activity 5-3: Choosing the Correct Meaning

Read each sentence below and think about what the word in italics means in the sentence. Then read the meanings for the word taken from a dictionary. The meanings shown are for one part of speech of the word. Use the context of the sentence to help you decide which meaning of the word is most appropriate for the sentence. Write this meaning in the space provided.

1. The movie was just another bit of *fluff* churned out by Hollywood.

   fluff n. 1. light down or fuzz, as on a young bird or on a dandelion. 2. something having a very light, soft, or frothy consistency or appearance. 3. something of little substance or consequence, especially light or superficial entertainment. 4. an error, especially in the delivery of lines as by an actor or an announcer.

   _____

2. Her loss in the election was a *signal* to her political party to seek a new candidate for the next election.

   signal n. 1. an indicator such as a gesture that serves as a means of communication. 2. something that incites action. 3. a fluctuating electric quantity such as current. 4. the sound, image, or message transmitted or received in television.

   _____

3. I always try to praise Susan because her self-image is extremely *delicate*.

   delicate adj. 1. fine in texture, quality, or construction. 2. fragile, easily broken or damaged. 3. hardly perceptible. 4. soft or faint.

   _____

4. The ability of animals to survive in the wild is largely a *function* of favorable climate and available food.

   function n. 1. the action for which one is particularly fitted or employed. 2. an assigned duty or activity. 3. an official ceremony or formal social occasion. 4. something closely related to another thing and dependent on it for its existence. 5. a mathematical variable related to another so that the value assumed by one is determined for the other.

   _____

157

Unit 5: Using Reference Sources

Activity 5-4: Thesaurus

Activity 5-4: Thesaurus

A *thesaurus*, whether print or online, is a reference source that contains synonyms for commonly used words. As noted in Activity 5-2, a synonym is a word that has the same or nearly the same meaning as another word. For example, "pale" is a synonym for "ashen."

A thesaurus is a very valuable tool to use in your writing. It can help you to avoid repeating the same words in monotonous fashion and to express yourself in an effective and interesting manner.

There are two ways in which a thesaurus may be arranged. Some print thesauruses are arranged by categories and subcategories. Almost all modern print thesauruses are arranged like a dictionary with entry words listed alphabetically. Synonyms are provided for all meanings and parts of speech of the entry word. When using an online thesaurus, you simply have to type in the word for which you want to identify synonyms.

Here a typical entry from a thesaurus (not all synonyms have been listed).

Entry Word: state
Part of Speech: noun
Definition: condition of mode or being
Synonyms: accompaniment, attitude, ...mood, nature, ...time, welfare

Entry Word: state
Part of Speech: noun
Definition: dignity, grandeur
Synonyms: cachet, ceremony, ...pomp, position, ...status, style

Entry Word: state
Part of Speech: noun
Definition: government, country
Synonyms: body politic, ...land, ...union

Entry Word: state
Part of Speech: verb
Definition: declare, assert
Synonyms: affirm, air, ...present, pronounce, ...ventilate, voice

Unit 5: Using Reference Sources

Activity 5-4: Thesaurus (continued)

You can see from the entry on the previous page that synonyms were provided for three definitions of *state* as a noun, as well as for one definition for *state* as a verb. Keep in mind that not all synonyms listed are identical. You will have to decide which synonym best fits your purpose. To help you do this, you may have to use a dictionary to look up the meanings of some of the words that are listed as synonyms in a thesaurus.

Keep in mind that a thesaurus has some limitations. The definitions provided for entry words in a thesaurus are not as complete and accurate as those found in a dictionary. You will find not as many entry words in a thesaurus as you will in a dictionary. The entry words in a thesaurus are typically only those words for which there are genuine alternatives with similar meanings. In many cases you will not find the technical or specialized sense of a word.

Answer the following questions about thesauruses.

1. What is the basic purpose of a thesaurus?

2. How are most modern thesauruses arranged?

3. What are two ways in which a thesaurus can be a valuable reference tool?

4. What is a synonym?

5. What does a thesaurus entry show if a word has more than one meaning?

6. What does a thesaurus entry show if a word has more than one part of speech?

7. What are three limitations of a thesaurus?

8. What should you do if you are not sure which synonym to use?

Unit 5: Using Reference Sources

Activity 5-5: Practice Using a Thesaurus

Activity 5-5: Practice Using a Thesaurus

For each of the sentences that follow, use a print or online thesaurus to find a synonym that you can use in place of the underlined word. Select the synonym that best matches the context of the sentence. Keep in mind that the underlined word may have more than one meaning and/or part of speech. Write the synonym you select on the blank line below the sentence.

1. I didn't mean to <u>imply</u> you were not capable of doing the job.

   _____

2. Henry was <u>prone</u> to getting angry when someone questioned his authority.

   _____

3. Elizabeth was absolutely <u>ebullient</u> when given the opportunity to act in the school play.

   _____

4. Samuel regarded the sudden drop in temperature as a <u>portent</u> of bad weather soon to come.

   _____

5. Juanita's mother felt that Juanita's reluctance to clean her room was yet another sign of her <u>contrary</u> nature.

   _____

6. I hope you will <u>indulge</u> my wish to see the movie again.

   _____

7. His <u>penitent</u> manner indicated that William felt guilty about what he had done.

   _____

8. Your idea is certainly <u>relevant</u> for this particular situation.

   _____

9. Your argument is so convincing that I am going to <u>embrace</u> your point of view.

   _____

10. Andrew was <u>stalwart</u> in the effort he put into preparing for the test.

    _____

Unit 5: Using Reference Sources

Activity 5-6: Choosing the Correct Synonym

Activity 5-6: Choosing the Correct Synonym

Here are some synonyms for the word *delivered*:

born, brought, ceded, declared, directed, discharged, gave, handed over, hurled, launched, presented, produced, provided, redeemed, rescued, resigned, surrendered, told, transferred, transmitted, transported

For each sentence below, write the synonym for *delivered* from the list above that best matches the context of the sentence.

1. The mailman _____ the package right to my door.

2. The message was _____ electronically via email.

3. The trapped mountain climbers were _____ from possible harm.

4. The general of the defeated army _____ the prisoners to the victorious army.

5. The baby was _____ just before midnight.

6. The mayor _____ his speech to the city council.

7. Andy _____ the ball fifty yards in the air right into waiting hands of the receiver.

8. The prisoner was _____ to the city hospital when his illness became extremely serious.

For each sentence below, circle the synonym that best replaces the underlined word.

9. Juanita was promoted because she was extremely competent.
   polished   knowing   proficient   suitable

10. Philip wanted to be sure that his business records were in a safe place.
    dependable   trustworthy   secure   discreet

11. Elizabeth wanted to be sure that she had adequate references for her research paper.
    decent   tolerable   fair   sufficient

12. The old man was quite well known for his strange habits.
    astounding   eccentric   alien   unfamiliar

Activity 5-7: Encyclopedia

An **encyclopedia** contains informative articles about subjects and often includes illustrations, maps, and photographs. The articles also often include definitions of key words and terms and references to additional information about a subject. Encyclopedias may be found in print and online formats.

With the advent of the Internet, many encyclopedias have discontinued print editions. Print editions of encyclopedias are typically very expensive and are mainly purchased by schools and libraries. Many online encyclopedias require the user to register and purchase a subscription. The free information provided by online encyclopedias is often limited in scope and depth.

Encyclopedias may be *general encyclopedias* or *subject encyclopedias*. A *general encyclopedia* provides information on a wide range of subjects. The articles they contain about a given subject are usually written by professional writers rather than experts on the subject and are not in-depth. General encyclopedias are useful if you are looking for a quick introduction to a subject. Well-known general encyclopedias include World Book and Britannica.

A *subject encyclopedia* contains articles devoted to a specific subject or area of interest, such as law or education. The articles are written by experts in the subject and are in-depth. You will find articles on specific topics within a subject. There are many subject encyclopedias. Two examples are the *Environmental Encyclopedia* and the *Encyclopedia of Philosophy*.

Wikipedia is a special case of a general encyclopedia and is available only online. It is a user-contributed encyclopedia. The articles found on Wikipedia are written collaboratively by unpaid Internet volunteers who often contribute anonymously or under a pseudonym. To a large extent, anyone with Internet access can make changes to the articles. However, a large core of volunteer editors regularly edit articles, helping to make the articles accurate and in a consistent style. Wikipedia identifies its best articles as Featured Articles and its second best tier of articles as Good Articles. The articles found on Wikipedia are continually created and updated. You may not find information you are looking for one day, yet you may find it the next day.

It is important to keep in mind that the articles found on Wikipedia are written largely by amateurs. Further, Wikipedia makes it very clear that it cannot vouch for the validity of the information found there. Technical, medical, and scientific articles are not subject to peer review by experts.

Unit 5: Using Reference Sources

Activity 5-7: Encyclopedia (continued)

Answer the following questions.

1. What are two types of encyclopedias?

2. What effect has the Internet had on the format of encyclopedias?

3. What does a general encyclopedia provide?

4. What does a subject encyclopedia provide?

5. Which type of encyclopedia should you use when you first begin to research a topic?

6. Which type of encyclopedia utilizes writers who are experts in their field of study?

7. What is Wikipedia?

8. Who write the articles that are found on Wikipedia?

9. Why should you be cautious when using Wikipedia?

10. If you are using a Wikipedia article as a reference when writing a paper, why should you frequently go back to look at that article?

Unit 5: Using Reference Sources

Activity 5-8: Almanac

Activity 5-8: Almanac

An **almanac** contains specific facts, statistical data, tables of comparative information, and organized lists of basic reference information related to people, places, events, etc. In addition to general almanacs such as the *World Almanac and Book of Facts*, there are subject almanacs such as sports almanacs, weather almanacs, and political almanacs.

Most almanacs are published yearly and continue to be primarily available in print editions. If you look at an almanac from year to year, each edition will appear to be quite similar. However, the information provided is updated from year to year. Almanacs include many specific facts that are difficult to find in any other type of reference source. Almanacs are available online although they vary in the amount of information they provide in this format, and are generally less comprehensive than are print almanacs.

Use the latest almanac available to answer the questions that follow. For each question, identify the name of the almanac in which you located the answer and check whether it was in a print or an online format.

1. Who was Secretary of Defense during the Carter administration?

   Answer: _____

   Name of almanac _____ Print _____ Online _____

2. Who was the recipient of the Noble Prize in chemistry in 1968?

   Answer: _____

   Name of almanac _____ Print _____ Online _____

3. What percentage of the popular vote did Clinton get when he was elected President in 1996?

   Answer: _____

   Name of almanac _____ Print _____ Online _____

4. What was the population of Green Bay, Wisconsin in 2000?

   Answer: _____

   Name of almanac _____ Print _____ Online _____

Unit 5: Using Reference Sources

Activity 5-8: Almanac (continued)

5. Which fast-food restaurant had the most franchises in 2010?

   Answer: _____

   Name of almanac _____ Print _____ Online _____

6. What is the name of the highest active volcano in Asia, and in what country is it located?

   Answer: _____

   Name of almanac _____ Print _____ Online _____

7. Which country won the gold medal in soccer at the 1960 Summer Olympics?

   Answer: _____

   Name of almanac _____ Print _____ Online _____

8. What is the length of the Nile River (in miles)?

   Answer: _____

   Name of almanac _____ Print _____ Online _____

9. What is the name and height of the highest dam in the United States?

   Answer: _____

   Name of almanac _____ Print _____ Online _____

10. Was the average size of a U.S. family greater in 1970 or in 2000?

    Answer: _____

    Name of almanac _____ Print _____ Online _____

Unit 5: Using Reference Sources

Activity 5-9: Statistical Abstract of the United States

Activity 5-9: Statistical Abstract of the United States

The *Statistical Abstract of the United States* is a publication of the United States Census Bureau, an agency of the United States Department of Commerce. Published annually since 1878, detailed statistics are provided to describe the social, political, and economic organization of the United States. Some international data is provided.

The abstract is available as a book, on a CD-ROM, and online. There is no registration or fee for use of the abstract online. You can access the abstract at http://www.census.gov/compendia/statab/. The information online is presented as tables in two formats: an Excel spreadsheet and a PDF file.

Use the latest version of the *Statistical Abstract of the United States* to answer the following questions.

1. How many electoral votes did the Democrats obtain in the South in the 1996 presidential election?

   _____

2. In 2007, how much more money did the average person whose highest degree was a Bachelor's degree earn than the average person whose highest degree was an Associate's degree?

   _____

3. What medical speciality had the greatest number of practitioners in 2000?

   _____

4. Which of these three food categories had the greatest production in terms of number of pounds in 2007: fruits, vegetables and melons, potatoes?

   _____

5. How many NCAA colleges had a men's basketball team in 2008?

   _____

   How many had a women's basketball team?

   _____

6. According to 2007 data, which ancestry group had the greatest representation in the total U.S. population?

   _____

Unit 5: Using Reference Sources

Activity 5-9: Statistical Abstract of the United States (continued)

7. How many more Sunday newspapers were there in 2000 than in 2008?

   _____

8. What percent of total sales of electronics and appliances were E-commerce sales in 2007?

   _____

9. Which of the following foods showed the greatest percentage increase in retail price per pound from 2000 to 2008: pork, dairy products, or cereal and bakery products?

   _____

10. How many new Broadway shows were produced from 2005 to 2007?

    _____

11. How many children ages 7-11 bowled in 2008?

    _____

12. Which airport was the busiest in 2008?

    _____

13. Which country had more carbon dioxide emissions in 2008: Finland or Hungary?

    _____

14. Does this abstract provide data about major league baseball?

    _____

15. Does it provide data about transportation?

    _____

Unit 5: Using Reference Sources

Activity 5-10: Atlas

Activity 5-10: Atlas

An **atlas** is a collection of maps. The two types of maps that you will use most often for school purposes are political maps and physical maps. A political map shows the governmental boundaries for regions such as countries, states, provinces, and counties. A physical map shows the geographic features of a region such as bodies of water, mountains, deserts, and plains.

Two comprehensive atlases that are in a print format are the *Atlas of the World* which is published by the Oxford University Press and the *National Geographic Atlas of the World*. Each contain many types of maps including political and physical maps. Many websites provide free access to maps as well.

Use an atlas in print form or maps found on the Internet to answer the following questions. After each answer, write the title of the print atlas or the name of the website that you used to locate your answer.

1. What four countries border France to the east?

    Answer: _____

    Title of atlas: _____

    Name of website: _____

2. Which country in South America extends furthest east?

    Answer: _____

    Title of atlas: _____

    Name of website: _____

3. What is the name of a desert in Africa?

    Answer: _____

    Title of atlas: _____

    Name of website: _____

4. Is Norway north or south of Denmark?

    Answer: _____

    Title of atlas: _____

    Name of website: _____

Unit 5: Using Reference Sources

Activity 5-10: Atlas (continued)

5. In which area of Australia is the Great Victoria Desert located – Southwest Australia or Northwest Australia?

   Answer: _____

   Title of atlas: _____

   Name of website: _____

6. Name the states that border Colorado.

   Answer: _____

   Title of atlas: _____

   Name of website: _____

7. What island nation lies due south of Cuba?

   Answer: _____

   Title of atlas: _____

   Name of website: _____

8. What country lies between Ireland and England?

   Answer: _____

   Title of atlas: _____

   Name of website: _____

9. What countries border the Black Sea?

   Answer: _____

   Title of atlas: _____

   Name of website: _____

10. In what ocean will you find the Philippines?

    Answer: _____

    Title of atlas: _____

    Name of website: _____

Unit 5: Using Reference Sources

Activity 5-11: Occupational Outlook Handbook

Activity 5-11: Occupational Outlook Handbook

As a high school student, your thinking about careers becomes important. The ***Occupational Outlook Handbook***, published every two years by the U.S. Department of Labor, is a valuable resource in this regard. For hundreds of different jobs, the handbook provides comprehensive information about the training and education needed, earnings, expected job prospects, details of the job, and the working conditions for that job. The handbook is available in book form, on a CD-ROM, and at the following website: http://www.bls.gov/oco/.

Use the most recent edition of the *Occupational Outlook Handbook* to answer the following questions.

1. What are the formal requirements for becoming a lawyer?

2. What are the three typical educational paths to becoming a registered nurse?

3. What was the average annual salary for anthropologists who worked for the Federal Government in 2009?

4. Is the number of postal service workers expected to increase or decrease over the next several years?

5. What is the primary job function of a correctional officer?

6. How many people were employed as pharmacists in 2008?

7. Who do most air traffic controllers work for?

8. If you join the U.S. Military, how many years must you serve to become eligible for retirement benefits?

Unit 5: Using Reference Sources

Activity 5-11: Occupational Outlook Handbook (continued)

9. Which states do not require special education teachers to be licensed?

_____

Select an occupation in which you have an interest. Use the *Occupational Outlook Handbook* to answer the following questions about that occupation.

10. What occupation did you select?

_____

11. What about the nature of the work appeals to you?

_____

_____

_____

_____

_____

12. What education, training, and liscensure are required?

_____

_____

13. What is the job outlook for the future?

_____

_____

14. Given your interest in the occupation you selected, what other occupations might you consider?

_____

15. After having read the information about the occupation you selected, has your interest in that occupation increased, decreased, or remained about the same?

_____

Unit 5: Using Reference Sources

Activity 5-12: What I Have Learned

Activity 5-12: What I Have Learned

Answer the following questions.

1. What five criteria should you use to evaluate information found on the Internet?

    _____

    _____

    _____

    _____

    _____

2. What are the two ways in which a thesaurus might be arranged?

    _____

    _____

3. Which type of encyclopedia contains articles written by experts in their subject fields?

    _____

4. What kind of information is provided when a dictionary describes the etymology of a word?

    _____

    _____

5. What are two purposes for which you might use a thesaurus?

    _____

    _____

6. How often is the *Occupational Outlook Handbook* published?

    _____

7. What publication should you use if you needed some highly detailed information about the United States economy?

    _____

Unit 5: Using Reference Sources

Activity 5-12: What I Have Learned (continued)

8. What is the difference between a political map and a physical map?

   _____

   _____

9. Which type of reference source is increasingly difficult to find in a print edition?

   _____

10. Does an online version of an almanac usually contain as much information as does a print version of an almanac?

    _____

Unit 6
Remembering Information

Activities

6-1   Repetition

6-2   Visualization

6-3   Categorization

6-4   Rhyme

6-5   Acronym

6-6   Acronymic Sentence

6-7   Pegwords

6-8   Keyword

6-9   Loci Strategy

6-10 What I Have Learned

Unit 6: Remembering Information

Activity 6-1: Repetition

Activity 6-1: Repetition

Repetition is a strategy for remembering facts in which you read, write, and say the facts to be remembered a number of times. It is a particularly useful strategy to use when you want to remember one or two facts.

Follow these steps to use the repetition strategy:

1. Read the fact(s) to be remembered.
2. Write the fact(s).
3. Say the fact(s).
4. Repeat the first three steps at least three times.

Here are the steps in the repetition strategy. For each step, write the missing word or words.

1. First, _____ the fact(s).
2. Second, _____ the fact(s).
3. Third, _____ the fact(s).
4. Finally, _____ the steps at least _____ times.

Use repetition to remember the following facts. Blank lines are provided for the writing you have to do in Step 2.

5. Fiji is located in the South Pacific Ocean.

_____

_____

_____

_____

Unit 6: Remembering Information

Activity 6-1: Repetition (continued)

6. The ocean contains three major environments: the neritic zone, the pelagic zone, and the benthic zone.

   _____
   _____
   _____
   _____

7. At the end of World War II, the United States, Britain, and France occupied the western portion of Germany.

   _____
   _____
   _____
   _____

8. Now, write some fact(s) from a textbook or from your class notes that you need to remember.

   _____
   _____
   _____
   _____

9. Use repetition to remember the fact(s) you wrote. Blank lines are provided for the writing you have to do in Step 2.

   _____
   _____
   _____
   _____

Unit 6: Remembering Information

Activity 6-2: Visualization

Activity 6-2: Visualization

Visualization is a strategy in which you create one or more pictures of something to be remembered in your mind. It is a good strategy for remembering information that is easy to picture.

Read the following selection about indoor air pollution, a significant environmental problem. As you read, create one or more pictures in your mind about the information presented. The picture(s) you create should be rich in detail to help you remember the important information about this environmental problem. Where possible, combine various aspects of the information in a picture to reduce the number of pictures you need to create to remember the information.

Indoor Air Pollution

Indoor air pollution is an increasing environmental problem in today's technological world. The escalating numbers and types of products and equipment used indoors in homes, such as portable heaters and aerosol sprays, give off fumes that may be dangerous. Because modern homes are so well insulated, the pollutants are trapped inside. These trapped pollutants often build to dangerous levels. People spend 90 percent of their time indoors. The people who spend the most time indoors are young children, old people, pregnant women, and people who are ill. These are the very people who are most likely to be harmed by pollutants. The problem is exacerbated if people smoke in their homes.

Describe the picture(s) you created in your mind as you read the selection about indoor air pollution.

1. _____

   _____

   _____

   _____

   _____

Compare your picture(s) with the description of a picture that a student created in her mind to remember the information about indoor air pollution. The student created a picture of a family gathering around the dining room table at sometime during the winter season. Gathered around the table are two parents, two grandparents, two young children, and an infant in a highchair. The father and grandmother are smoking while the mother is spraying a deodorizer to get rid of the smell. A portable heater in the corner of the room is set to high heat.

Unit 6: Remembering Information

Activity 6-2: Visualization (continued)

Read the following information about basic food groups.

Basic Food Groups

Good nutrition leads to good health. The United States Department of Agriculture (USDA) categorizes foods into five basic food groups. It is important to include all five of the basic food groups in your diet. Here are the five basic food groups and examples of each.

Grains: Cheerios, Wonder Bread, spaghetti

Fruits: pears, oranges

Vegetables: peas, lettuce, potatoes

Dairy: milk, swiss cheese, yogurt

Meat, Poultry, Fish, Dry Beans, Eggs, and Nuts: fried chicken, plain omelette, peanuts

In addition, it is important to include some fats, oils, and sweets in your diet.

Describe the picture(s) you created in your mind as you read the information about basic food groups.

2. _____

_____

_____

_____

_____

Unit 6: Remembering Information

Activity 6-2: Visualization (continued)

Use a sheet of paper to cover the information that was provided on the previous page about basic food groups. Use the picture(s) you created in your mind to answer the following questions.

3. What are the five USDA basic food groups?

   _____

   _____

   _____

   _____

   _____

4. To which basic food group do each of the following belong?

   potatoes _____

   swiss cheese _____

   spaghetti _____

5. Now, copy a paragraph from one of your textbooks in the space provided here.

   _____

   _____

   _____

   _____

   _____

   _____

6. Describe the picture(s) you would create in your mind to remember the important information provided in the paragraph.

   _____

   _____

   _____

   _____

   _____

Unit 6: Remembering Information

Activity 6-3: Categorization

Activity 6-3: Categorization

Categorization is a strategy for remembering items of information that can be sorted into two or more categories.

Follow these steps to use the categorization strategy.

1. Look for ways in which the items of information to be remembered can be sorted into two or more categories.

2. Write the name for each category as a heading.

3. Under the heading for the first category, write each item of information that belongs to that category.

4. Repeat Step 3 for each of the other categories.

Here is an example to show how categorization is used.

Suppose you have to remember the following items that are typically found in a supermarket: orange juice, white bread, milk, onions, English muffins, lettuce, cookies, soda, dinner rolls, and cucumbers.

First, in your mind, think of how these items can be sorted into categories of supermarket items. In this example, these categories would be baked goods, drinks, and vegetables. Second, write the name for each category as a heading. Third, under the heading Baked Goods, write the name of each item that is a baked good. Fourth, repeat this for items that belong in the Drinks category, and then for items that belong in the Vegetables category.

This is what you would have:

Baked Goods	Drinks	Vegetables
white bread	orange juice	onions
English muffins	milk	lettuce
cookies	soda	cucumbers
dinner rolls		

To remember all of the items, think of the first category, Baked Goods. You will remember white bread, English muffins, cookies, and dinner rolls. Then do the same for Drinks and then for Vegetables.

Unit 6: Remembering Information

Activity 6-3: Categorization (continued)

Use the categorization strategy to remember the following sources of pollution in the environment: ovens, automobiles, liquid detergent, stoves, trucks, bleach, furniture polish, airplanes, ships, and gas barbecues.

1. Organize these sources of pollution into categories. Write a heading for each category of pollution. Then, write each source of pollution below the heading for the category to which it belongs.

    Category _____   _____   _____

    Source   _____   _____   _____

             _____   _____   _____

             _____   _____   _____

             _____   _____   _____

2. Now, locate in a textbook or your class notes some items of information that you need to remember. Select items that you can sort into two or more categories. Write the items here.

    _____

    _____

    _____

    _____

    _____

    _____

3. Write the headings of categories under which you can group the items. Under each heading, write the items that belong in that category.

    Category _____   _____   _____

    Source   _____   _____   _____

             _____   _____   _____

             _____   _____   _____

             _____   _____   _____

Unit 6: Remembering Information

Activity 6-4: Rhyme

Activity 6-4: Rhyme

Rhyme is a strategy for remembering information in which you create lines of verse that have corresponding sounds at their ends. That is, the ends of each line rhyme with each other. Here is an example of how rhyme is used to remember information.

In fourteen hundred ninety two

Columbus sailed the ocean blue.

These lines of verse rhyme because the last word in the first line (two) has the same sound as the last word in the second line (blue).

Here is an example of how you can use rhyme to remember a social studies fact.

There are four states whose names start with New.

New Hampshire and New Mexico are just two.

New York and New Jersey complete the four.

I'm sure there aren't any more.

You do not have to be a poet to use rhyme. Have fun and let your imagination run wild. Here is an example of using a longer rhyme to remember facts about two former presidents of the United States.

Here's a fact just as a starter.

Our 39th president was Jimmy Carter.

Now here's another as we're parting.

Our 29th president was Warren Harding.

Write two or four lines of rhyming verse to remember the following information.

1. Iron has to be extracted from its ore by a process called smelting.

_____

_____

_____

_____

Unit 6: Remembering Information

Activity 6-4: Rhyme (continued)

2. Saturn is the second largest planet in our solar system, yet it is the lightest.

3. A zebra is part of the horse family.

4. The first maps were drawn on tablets of clay.

5. Zinc and nickel, along with copper, are commonly used as alloys to make coins.

6. Frogs are related to toads, but frogs have a slimmer body while toads have drier skin.

Unit 6: Remembering Information

Activity 6-4: Rhyme (continued)

7. High school graduates earn less than college graduates, and high school drop-outs earn even less.

   _____
   _____
   _____
   _____

8. New York City is the most populated city in the United States. Do you know that 36% of its population was born outside of the United States?

   _____
   _____
   _____
   _____

9. Now, write some information you have to remember from a textbook or from your class notes.

   _____
   _____
   _____
   _____

10. Write two or four lines of rhyming verse to remember this information.

    _____
    _____
    _____
    _____

Unit 6: Remembering Information

Activity 6-5: Acronym

Activity 6-5: Acronym

Acronym is a strategy for remembering information in which you form a word by using the first letter of each item of information to be remembered. The acronym you form can be a real word or a nonsense word you are able to pronounce. Acronym is a good strategy to use when the information to be remembered does not have to be remembered in a certain order. It is often difficult to form an acronym when you have to remember information in a certain order.

Follow these steps to form an acronym.

> 1. Write each item of information you need to remember.
>
> 2. Underline the first letter of each item of information to be remembered. If there is more than one word in an item of information, underline the first letter of only the first word.
>
> 3. Arrange the underlined letters to form an acronym that is a real word or a nonsense word that you can pronounce.

"CAGED" is an example of an acronym that is a real word you can use to remember the names of the following five famous scientists in any order: Einstein, Copernicus, Galileo, Archimedes, and Darwin. In CAGED, "C" is the first letter of Copernicus, "A" is the first letter of Archimedes, and so on. Whenever you must remember the names of these five scientists, think of the acronym CAGED. The "C" in CAGED will help you recall that Copernicus is one of these scientists, the "A" will help you recall Archimedes, and so on.

"Petil" is an acronym that can be used to remember the names of the following five inventions in any order: elevator, ice cream, laser, television, and parachute. "Petil" is not a real word, but you can easily pronounce it. Notice that you cannot form a real word from the first letter of each of the inventions to be remembered.

Sometimes, two or more of the items of information you must remember each begins with the same letter. The acronym "ratt" can be used to remember the following four types of dinosaurs in any order: triceratops, apatosaurus, tyrannosaurus rex, and stegosaurus. You can use the first letter "t" in this acronym to remember either "triceratops" or "tyrannosaurus rex," and the second letter "t" to remember the other.

Unit 6: Remembering Information

Activity 6-5: Acronym (continued)

Write an acronym for each of the following sets of items of information. The items of information in each set can be remembered in any order. Your acronym can be a real word or a nonsense word you are able to pronounce. For each set of information, use a real word if possible.

1. *Countries:* Haiti, Argentina, Cyprus, Thailand

   _____

2. *Languages:* French, German, English, Spanish

   _____

3. *Native American Tribes:* Apache, Comanche, Pequot, Sioux

   _____

4. *Elements:* radium, aluminum, lithium, oxygen, phosphorus

   _____

5. *Birds:* toucan, avocet, eagle, swift, egret

   _____

6. *Computer and Internet Terms:* user interface, motherboard, hyperlink, encryption, spreadsheet program

   _____

7. *Horse breeds:* Palomino, Egyptian, Appaloosa, Paso Fino, Lipizzan.

   _____

8. *Fish:* red fin, kennyi, elephant nose, betta, angel.

   _____

9. Now, write some items of information from a textbook or from your class notes that can be remembered in any order.

   _____

   _____

10. Write an acronym to remember this information.

    _____

Unit 6: Remembering Information

Activity 6-6: Acronymic Sentence

Activity 6-6: Acronymic Sentence

Acronymic sentence is a strategy that is equally useful for remembering information in any order or remembering information in a certain order. It is similar to the acronym strategy you learned about in Activity 6-5. The difference is that the first letter of each item of information to be remembered is used to create a sentence rather than form a word.

Follow these steps to use the acronymic sentence strategy.

---

1. Write each item of information you need to remember. Write these in any order or in a certain order if required.

2. Underline the first letter of each item of information.

3. Write a sentence using words that begin with the underlined letters.

Try to create a sentence that is funny or is personal to you. You will find it easier to remember the sentence if you do this.

Here is an example of an acronymic sentence that was created to remember the following four occupations *in any order:* teacher, accountant, chemist, lawyer.

   Adam loves cinnamon tea.

Here is an example of the use of an acronymic sentence to remember information *in a certain order*. In this example, the information to be remembered is four manufactured products exported by the United States in order from highest to lowest in dollar value of the exports. The exported products in this order are as follows: electrical machinery, vehicles, scientific instruments, ships.

In this example, the order of the products cannot be changed from that shown. Here is an acronymic sentence that was created to show these products in the required order.

   Edith values salami sandwiches.

Because two of the manufactured goods to be remembered each begins with the letter "s," you will have to later recall that "salami" stands for scientific instruments and that "sandwiches" stands for ships.

Unit 6: Remembering Information

Activity 6-6: Acronymic Sentence (continued)

Write an acronymic sentence to remember each of the following.

1. Five world capitals in any order: Copenhagen, New Delhi, Warsaw, London, Madrid.

_____

2. Five national parks in order of size from the smallest acreage to the largest acreage.

Wind Cave	28,295 acres
Grand Canyon	1,217403 acres
Everglades	1,508,538 acres
Glacier	1,013,572 acres
Rocky Mountain	265,828 acres

3. Five categories of Nobel Prize awards in any order: physics, chemistry, medicine, literature, peace.

_____

4. Six major natural lakes of the world in order of their maximum depth in feet from the deepest to the shallowest.

Great Bear	1,463 feet
Albert	168 feet
Ontario	802 feet
Tanganyika	4,823 feet
Baykal	5,315 feet
Onega	328 feet

_____

5. Five famous entertainers in order of their dates of birth from earliest to most recent.

Elvis Presley	1935
James Dean	1931
John Wayne	1907
Paul Newman	1925
Bruce Springsteen	1949

_____

Unit 6: Remembering Information

Activity 6-6: Acronymic Sentence (continued)

6. Six major industries in Pennsylvania in any order: travel, health care, publishing, biotechnology, legal services, trucking.

   _____

7. The average SAT combined scores for Critical Reading, Writing, and Math for states in 2010 in order from the state with the highest score to the state with the lowest.

Oklahoma	1684
North Carolina	1485
Missouri	1768
Arizona	1544
Pennsylvania	1473

   _____

8. Now, write some items of information from a textbook or from your class notes that must be remembered in any order.

   _____

   _____

   _____

9. Write an acronymic sentence to remember these items of information.

   _____

10. This time, write some items of information from a textbook or from your class notes that must be remembered in a certain order.

    _____

    _____

    _____

11. Write an acronymic sentence to remember these items of information.

    _____

Activity 6-7: Pegwords

Pegwords is a strategy that is useful for remembering numbered information, such as the four most important reasons for going to college or the first three amendments to the Constitution of the United States. Pegwords are words that rhyme with a number word. Each pegword is substituted for a number word and is then associated with the information to be remembered.

Here are suggested pegwords for the number words one through ten. For most purposes, you will not need more than ten pegwords. You can substitute your own pegwords if you wish. Nouns or verbs are best to use as pegwords since they can easily be used to form many associations with the information to be remembered.

Number Word	Pegword
one	run
two	shoe
three	tree
four	door
five	hive
six	sticks
seven	heaven
eight	gate
nine	sign
ten	pen

Follow these steps to use the pegwords strategy:

1. Think of the first item of information you must remember.

2. Think of the pegword for the number word *one*. The pegword for *one* is *run*.

3. Form an association in your mind between the pegword *run* and the first item of information you must remember.

4. Create a picture in your mind of this association.

5. Repeat steps 1-4 for each additional item of information you must remember. Use the pegword *shoe* for the second item, *tree* for the third item, and so on.

Unit 6: Remembering Information

Activity 6-7: Pegwords (continued)

Here is an example of how the pegwords strategy is used to remember the first two rights granted under the Bill of Rights. The first right is "freedom of religion." To remember this first right, associate freedom of religion with the pegword *run*. For example, you could create a picture in your mind in which people are *running* out of a church and are being chased by armed soldiers to prevent them from observing their religion. Later, when you try to remember the first right under the Bill of Rights, the number word *one* will trigger the pegword *run*, which will in turn trigger your mental picture of people running out of a church and being chased by soldiers—that is, freedom of religion is the first right under the Bill of Rights.

The second right is that "states can have a national guard." You can remember this by using the pegword *shoe* to create a mental picture such as armed soldiers guarding a giant shoe.

Now, describe the pictures you would create in your mind using the pegword strategy to remember the third through the fifth rights granted under the Bill of Rights.

1. Third Right: We do not have to give food or shelter to soldiers during peacetime.

   _____
   _____
   _____

2. Fourth Right: Our homes cannot be searched without a search warrant signed by a judge.

   _____
   _____
   _____

3. Fifth Right: We cannot be deprived of life, liberty, or property without due process of law.

   _____
   _____
   _____

Unit 6: Remembering Information

Activity 6-7: Pegwords (continued)

4. Now, write some information from a textbook or from your class notes for which pegwords would be a good strategy to use.

_____
_____
_____
_____
_____

5. For each pegword you use, describe the picture you would create in your mind to remember the information that is associated with that pegword.

_____
_____
_____
_____
_____
_____
_____
_____
_____
_____

Unit 6: Remembering Information

Activity 6-8: Keyword

Activity 6-8: Keyword

Keyword is a strategy that is useful for remembering the meanings of new and difficult words you find in your textbooks and hear in class. A keyword is a word whose meaning you already know and that sounds like the entire word or a major part of a word whose meaning you need to remember.

Follow these steps to use the keyword strategy:

1. Change the word whose meaning you need to remember into a keyword. Your keyword should be a word whose meaning you know and that sounds like the entire word or a major part of the word whose meaning you must remember.

2. Create a picture in your mind that relates your keyword to the meaning of the word whose meaning you must remember.

3. Think of your keyword for the word whose meaning you must remember and then recall the picture you created in your mind.

Here is an example of how the keyword strategy can be used to remember the meaning of *ellipse* (an ellipse is a flattened circle).

First, change the word *ellipse* into the keyword *lips*. The keyword *lips* is a word whose meaning you know and that sounds like a major part of *ellipse*. Second, create a picture in your mind of someone leaning toward you to kiss you. This person's lips are shaped like a flattened circle. Third, think of your keyword *lips* and the picture you created. Picturing someone with flattened lips who is about to kiss you will help you to remember that an ellipse is a flattened circle.

Use the keyword strategy to remember the meaning given for each of the following words. If you need to, use a print dictionary or an online dictionary to help you pronounce the word. For each word, write your keyword and then describe the picture you would create in your mind.

1. *centurion:* a commander in the army of ancient Rome.

   Keyword _____

   Picture _____

Unit 6: Remembering Information

Activity 6-8: Keyword (continued)

2. *obfuscate:* to make something so confusing that it is difficult to understand.

   Keyword _____

   Picture _____

3. *gurney:* a metal stretcher with wheeled legs, used for transporting patients.

   Keyword _____

   Picture _____

4. *regale:* to entertain or provide with great enjoyment.

   Keyword _____

   Picture _____

5. Write a word from your textbook or class notes whose meaning you do not know but have to remember.

   _____

6. Use a print or online dictionary to learn the meaning of the word. Write the meaning here.

   _____

7. Write the keyword you would use to remember the meaning of the word.

   _____

8. Describe the picture you would create in your mind.

   _____

   _____

   _____

Activity 6-9: Loci Strategy

The word *locus* means place. *Loci* is the plural form of locus. It is easy to remember features of places with which you are familiar, such as where you live or your school. The **loci** strategy builds on your familiarity with a place. It is an effective strategy to use to remember information if you are good at visualizing things.

Here is how to use the loci strategy for information that can be remembered in any order.

1. Think of a place you know very well.
2. Visualize the features of that place.
3. Visualize each item of information you want to remember and associate it with one of the features of that place.
4. Visualize each feature you selected and the item of information you associated with it to recall the information you want to remember.

For example, suppose for a history class you need to remember what each of the following Roman goddesses represents.

Venus	Goddess of love and beauty.
Minerva	Goddess of wisdom.
Juventas	Goddess of youth.
Vesta	Goddess of hearth and home.
Patalena	Goddess of flowers.

You decide to use your favorite shopping mall as the familiar place. You use stores in the mall as features. Here is what you might visualize for each goddess.

Venus	A cosmetics store. (beauty)
Minerva	A book store. (wisdom)
Juventas	A toy store. (youth)
Vesta	A furniture store. (home)
Patalena	A flower shop or kiosk. (flowers)

To recall what a goddess represents, visualize the store you associated with that goddess. For example, to recall what Venus represents, visualize a store in the mall that sells cosmetics and various beauty aids.

Unit 6: Remembering Information

Activity 6-9: Loci Strategy (continued)

Complete the following.

1. You are studying types of phobias in your psychology class. Use the loci strategy to remember what each of the following types of phobia is. Use the place you live in as the place you are very familiar with.

bibliophobia	fear of books
photophobia	fear of light
dendrophobia	fear of trees
cathisophobia	fear of sitting
chronophobia	fear of time
mysophobia	fear of germs

For each phobia, identify a feature of the place you live in and describe what you visualized in your mind to remember the phobia you associated with that feature.

bibliophobia

Feature: _____

What I visualized: _____

_____

photophobia

Feature: _____

What I visualized: _____

_____

dendrophobia

Feature: _____

What I visualized: _____

_____

cathisophobia

Feature: _____

What I visualized: _____

_____

_____

chronophobia

Feature: _____

What I visualized: _____

_____

_____

mysophobia

Feature: _____

What I visualized: _____

_____

_____

In the example previously shown for Roman goddesses, and in the exercise you just completed for phobias, you could remember the information in any order. You can also use the loci strategy to remember items of information in a certain order, although the loci strategy is used more frequently for information that can be remembered in any order.

When using the loci strategy to remember items of information in a certain order, use the features of a familiar place in a logical order. Think of the example that was shown of using a shopping mall as a familiar place to remember what each of five Roman goddesses represents. This time you must remember what each goddess represents in the order shown.

Venus	Goddess of love and beauty.
Minerva	Goddess of wisdom.
Juventas	Goddess of youth.
Vesta	Goddess of hearth and home.
Patalena	Goddess of flowers.

Unit 6: Remembering Information

Activity 6-9: Loci Strategy (continued)

To do this, think of the first five stores you come to when you enter the mall from the entrance you usually use. Here are the stores in the order in which you would come to them.

  A clothing store.

  A crafts store.

  A bath and bodyworks store.

  An athletic footwear store.

  An electronics store.

You will have be more creative in the associations you make between the goddesses and the stores. You might visualize Venus looking beautiful in a new dress she has tried on in the clothing store, Minerva looking through a book about the history of candlemaking in the crafts store, and so on.

Complete the following.

2. Once again, use the loci strategy to remember what each of the following types of phobias is. Continue to use the place you live in as a place with which you are familiar. However, this time you must remember what each phobia is in the alphabetical order of the phobias as shown. Remember that the features you use must be in some kind of logical order.

bibliophobia	fear of books
cathisophobia	fear of sitting
chronophobia	fear of time
dendrophobia	fear of trees
mysophobia	fear of germs
photophobia	fear of light

bibliophobia

Feature: _____

What I visualized: _____

_____

_____

Unit 6: Remembering Information

Activity 6-9: Loci Strategy (continued)

cathisophobia

Feature: _____

What I visualized: _____
_____
_____

chronophobia

Feature: _____

What I visualized: _____
_____
_____

dendrophobia

Feature: _____

What I visualized: _____
_____
_____

mysophobia

Feature: _____

What I visualized: _____
_____
_____

photophobia

Feature: _____

What I visualized: _____
_____
_____

Unit 6: Remembering Information

Activity 6-9: Loci Strategy (continued)

3. Now, write six items of information from a textbook or from your class notes that can be remembered in any order.

   _____
   _____
   _____
   _____
   _____

4. Write the name of the familiar place you are using.

   _____

5. Complete the following for the information you must remember.

   First item to remember: _____

   Feature: _____

   What I visualized: _____
   _____
   _____

   Second item to remember: _____

   Feature: _____

   What I visualized: _____
   _____
   _____

   Third item to remember: _____

   Feature: _____

   What I visualized: _____
   _____
   _____

Unit 6: Remembering Information

Activity 6-9: Loci Strategy (continued)

Fourth item to remember: _____

Feature: _____

What I visualized: _____

_____

_____

Fifth item to remember: _____

Feature: _____

What I visualized: _____

_____

_____

Sixth item to remember: _____

Feature: _____

What I visualized: _____

_____

_____

Unit 6: Remembering Information

Activity 6-10: What I Have Learned

Activity 6-10: What I Have Learned

In this unit, you have learned about nine strategies for remembering information. Complete each of the following by writing the name of the remembering strategy that is being used by the student. Use each strategy just once.

1. Roberta must remember that Wyoming is known as the "Cowboy State." She writes this fact and recites it several times.

    The strategy Roberta is using is _____.

2. Helene must remember the events in a story about the accidental discovery of an unusual galaxy. She creates pictures in her mind as she reads the story.

    The strategy Helene is using is _____.

3. Edgar must remember to bring the following ten items with him on a field trip to the Grand Canyon: hairbrush, books, tent, nail clipper, wooden matches, razor, portable CD player, cologne, harmonica, and sleeping bag. He groups these items under the following headings: Grooming Items, Camping Items, and Recreational Items.

    The strategy Edgar is using is _____.

4. Dolores must remember the meaning of the word "interlude." She does not know the meaning of this word, but she associates it with the word "prelude," whose meaning she does know.

    The strategy Dolores is using is _____.

5. William must remember the names of these four famous philosophers in any order: Plato, Confucius, Aristotle, and Sartre. He uses the first letter of the name of each philosopher to form the word CAPS.

    The strategy William is using is _____.

6. Tyler must remember the following four effects of the industrial revolution: (1) cities grew rapidly as people began to leave the countryside to find work, (2) industrialization spread widely across the world, (3) people enjoyed higher standards of living, and (4) environmental pollution increased. He associates these effects with words that rhyme with the number words one through four.

    The strategy Tyler is using is _____.

Unit 6: Remembering Information

Activity 6-10: What I Have Learned (continued)

7. Susan must remember the following five fruits as shown in their order of Vitamin A content, from highest content to lowest: cantaloupe, apricot, watermelon, peach, and orange. She forms the following sentence using words that begin with the first letter of each of these fruits in the order shown: Can apes wear pink orchids?

   The strategy Susan is using is _____.

8. Javier is taking a class in economics. He needs to remember the following high-paying careers: investment banker, software developer, actuary, engineer, nurse. Javier associates each career with a feature found in his school.

   The strategy Javier is using is _____.

9. Samuel must remember that St. Augustine, Florida was founded in 1565 by Francis Drake. To remember this information, he created several lines of verse using words with corresponding sounds at the end of each pair of lines.

   The strategy Samuel is using is _____.

Now answer these questions.

10. Is the acronym strategy a good strategy to use when you have to remember information in a certain order?

    _____

11. Which strategy is particularly good to use when you have to remember numbered information such as the four reasons dinosaurs became extinct?

    _____

12. Which strategy is particularly useful for remembering information that is easy to picture?

    _____

13. There are a number of things you have to bring to school for a project. These things fall into several groups. Which strategy should you use to remember these?

    _____

14. Which strategy do you think Henry Wadsworth Longfellow would find appealing?

    _____

Unit 7
Graphic Organizers and Charts

Activities

7-1   Topic-List Graphic Organizer

7-2   Series of Events Graphic Organizer

7-3   Compare-Contrast Graphic Organizer

7-4   Problem-Solution Graphic Organizer

7-5   Question-Answer Graphic Organizer

7-6   Cause-Effect Graphic Organizer

7-7   Series of Steps Chart

7-8   Five W's Chart

7-9   KWL Chart

7-10 What I Have Learned

Unit 7: Graphic Organizers and Charts

Activity 7-1: Topic-List Graphic Organizer

Activity 7-1: Topic-List Graphic Organizer

Graphic organizers and charts are visual representations of information. They can help you to understand and remember information. You will be learning about nine graphic organizers and charts in this unit.

A **topic-list** graphic organizer can help you to organize information about a topic into its subtopics and details.

Read the following information about Amelia Earhart.

> Amelia Earhart, born in 1897, remains the most famous female aviator in history. She learned to fly early in 1921 and bought her first plane, a Kinner Canary, later that year. She used this plane to set a women's record by reaching an altitude of 14,000 feet in 1922. In 1928, Earhart became the first woman to fly across the Atlantic Ocean. On this flight, she was a passenger in a plane piloted by Wilmer Stutz and Louis Gordon. In 1932, Earhart became the first woman and only the second person to fly solo across the Atlantic. She flew her Lockheed Vega from Newfoundland to Ireland in just less than fifteen hours, bettering the time it took Charles Lindbergh to make the first solo flight across the Atlantic in 1927. In 1935, Earhart became the first person to fly solo across the Pacific Ocean from Hawaii to California. In 1937, she sought to become the first woman to fly around the world. Along with her navigator, Fred Noonan, she set out from Miami, Florida. After completing more than two-thirds of the flight, their plane vanished in the central Pacific near the International Date Line. Extensive search efforts were unsuccessful. The exact nature of Earhart's and Noonan's disappearance remains a mystery, although there is speculation that Earhart might have survived a crash and lived out her life as a castaway on a remote Pacific island.

On the next page is a topic-list graphic organizer a student constructed based on the information provided about Amelia Earhart. It illustrates how a topic-list graphic organizer is constructed.

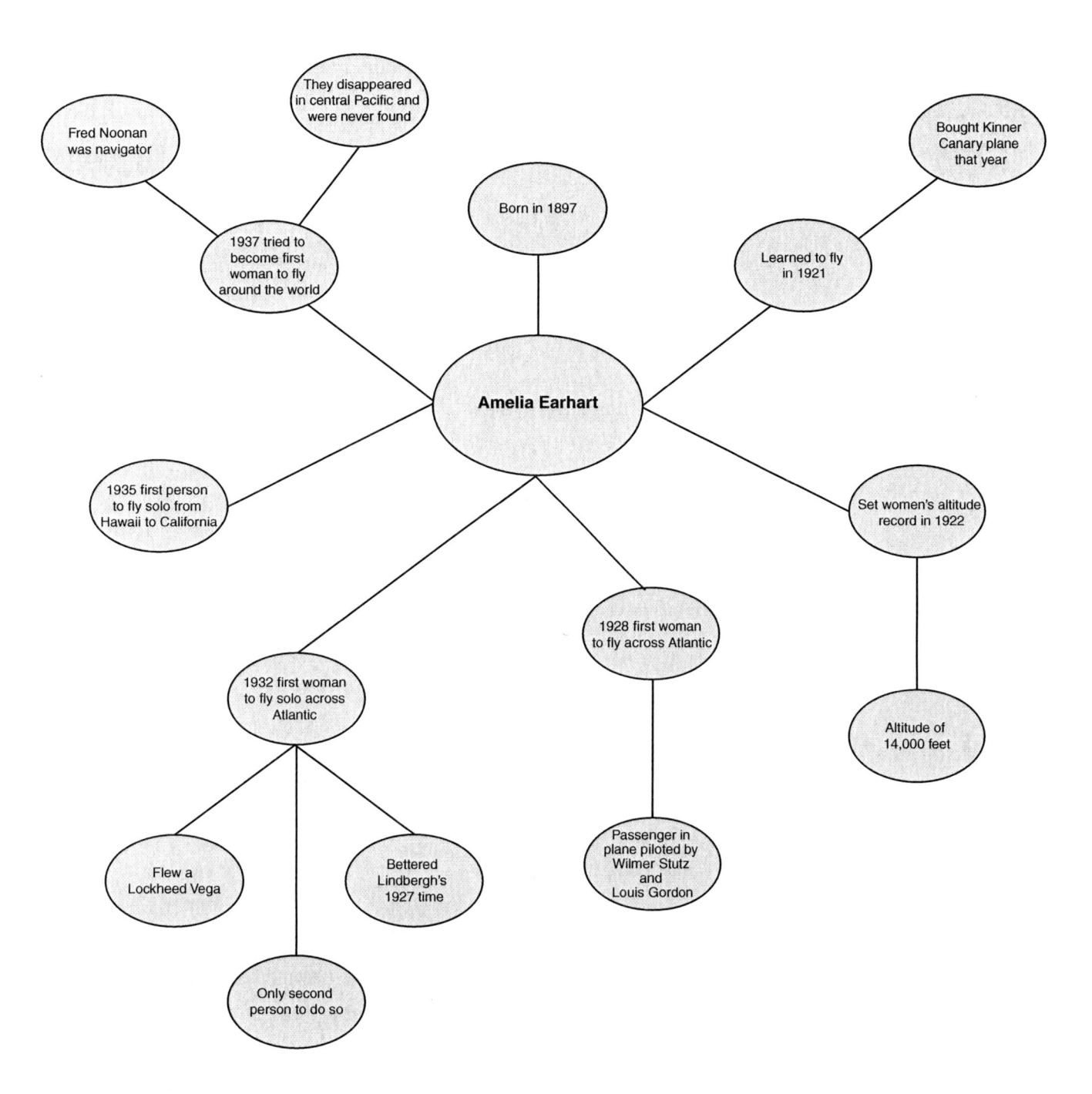

Unit 7: Graphic Organizers and Charts

Activity 7-1: Topic-List Graphic Organizer (continued)

Amelia Earhart

- Born in 1897
- Learned to fly in 1921
  - Bought Kinner Canary plane that year
- Set women's altitude record in 1922
  - Altitude of 14,000 feet
- 1928 first woman to fly across Atlantic
  - Passenger in plane piloted by Wilmer Stutz and Louis Gordon
- 1932 first woman to fly solo across Atlantic
  - Flew a Lockheed Vega
  - Bettered Lindbergh's 1927 time
  - Only second person to do so
- 1935 first person to fly solo from Hawaii to California
- 1937 tried to become first woman to fly around the world
  - Fred Noonan was navigator
  - They disappeared in central Pacific and were never found

Unit 7: Graphic Organizers and Charts

Activity 7-1: Topic-List Graphic Organizer (continued)

Read the following information about the Erie Canal.

> The Erie Canal is a historic waterway whose construction began in 1817 and was completed in 1825. It stretched from Buffalo, New York on Lake Erie to Albany, New York on the Hudson River. Construction was difficult and required 83 locks to move boats up and down natural elevations and 18 aqueducts to carry the canal over bodies of water. The canal was an instant commercial success. The cost of transporting products from Buffalo to New York City by canal boats that were pulled by mules or horses was much lower than the cost of doing so by wagons. The canal facilitated two-way trade between New York City and Midwestern states and Canada. Farm goods came east while manufactured goods went west. The canal was enlarged in 1862 so that boats could carry more goods. It was enlarged again in 1915 so that it could handle steamships and was renamed the New York State Barge Canal. Traffic on the canal dwindled with the development of railroads and the St. Lawrence Seaway. Now known as the New York State Canalway Trail, more than 200 miles of the Barge Canal and the original Erie Canal are used for multipurpose recreation.

Now, construct a topic-list graphic organizer about this information on the blank page that follows.

Unit 7: Graphic Organizers and Charts

Activity 7-1: Topic-List Graphic Organizer (continued)

Construct your topic-list graphic organizer here.

Unit 7: Graphic Organizers and Charts

Activity 7-2: Series of Events Graphic Organizer

Activity 7-2: Series of Events Graphic Organizer

A series of events graphic organizer is useful when studying historical information. It allows you to show the order in which events occurred along with important details about each event.

Read the following information about the French and Indian War.

> The French and Indian War had to do with the contest between France and England for control of North America. Although battles between the French along with their Indian allies and the British had been occurring for several years, it wasn't until 1756 that war was officially declared. Military activity that year and the following year was relatively inconclusive, although the French generally had the better of it. Things began to change in 1758. That summer, the British captured Louisbourg, Nova Scotia from the French. This established British control of the Bay of St. Lawrence. Later that year, the British captured Fort Frontenac at the eastern end of Lake Ontario. The British now controlled Lake Ontario. They then established peace with the Indian tribes of the region. With their Indians allies lost to them, the French abandoned Fort Duquesne to the British, thereby relinquishing their control of the upper Ohio Valley. The British renamed it Fort Pitt. In 1759, the British continued to capture French forts, including Fort Niagara. Later that year, in the largest attack of the war, the British captured Quebec. In 1760, the British captured Montreal and Detroit, virtually eliminating French influence in North America. The war came to an official end in 1763 with the signing of the Treaty of Paris. France ceded all of North America east of the Mississippi, with the exception of New Orleans, to England. As part of the treaty, France also turned over its claims to New Orleans and all lands west of the Mississippi to Spain.

Unit 7: Graphic Organizers and Charts

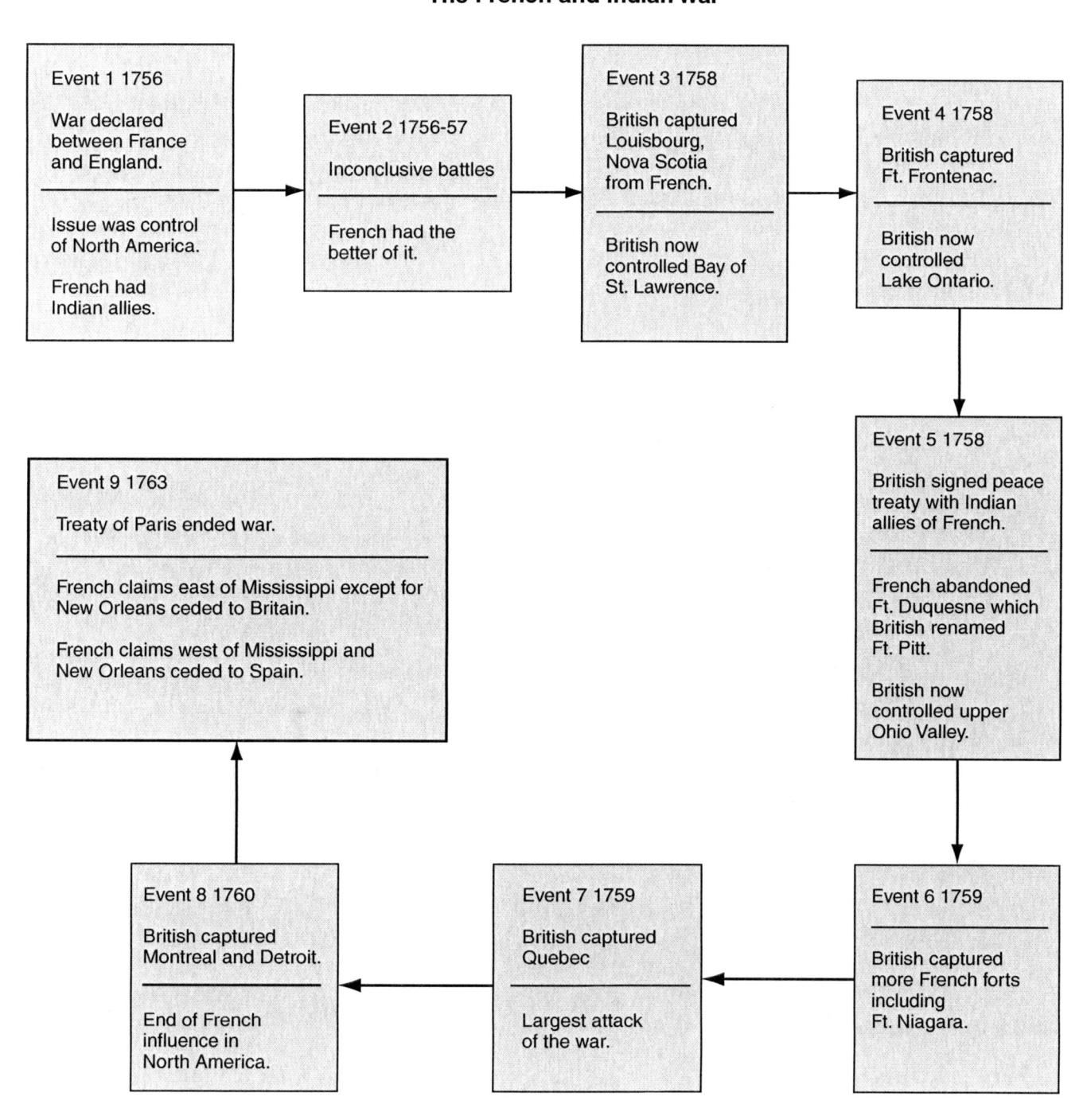

Activity 7-2: Series of Events Graphic Organizer (continued)

Look at the series of events graphic organizer a student constructed based on the information provided about the French and Indian War. This illustrates how a series of events graphic organizer is constructed.

The French and Indian War

Event 1 1756
War declared between France and England.
Issue was control of North America.
French had Indian allies.

→

Event 2 1756-57
Inconclusive battles
French had the better of it.

→

Event 3 1758
British captured Louisbourg, Nova Scotia from French.
British now controlled Bay of St. Lawrence.

→

Event 4 1758
British captured Ft. Frontenac.
British now controlled Lake Ontario.

↓

Event 5 1758
British signed peace treaty with Indian allies of French.
French abandoned Ft. Duquesne which British renamed Ft. Pitt.
British now controlled upper Ohio Valley.

↓

Event 6 1759
British captured more French forts including Ft. Niagara.

←

Event 7 1759
British captured Quebec
Largest attack of the war.

←

Event 8 1760
British captured Montreal and Detroit.
End of French influence in North America.

↑

Event 9 1763
Treaty of Paris ended war.
French claims east of Mississippi except for New Orleans ceded to Britain.
French claims west of Mississippi and New Orleans ceded to Spain.

Unit 7: Graphic Organizers and Charts

Activity 7-2: Series of Events Graphic Organizer (continued)

Read the following information about the first voyage of Christopher Columbus.

> The first voyage of Columbus to the New World was actually a misguided attempt to reach Asia by sailing over what was presumed to be open sea. With the sponsorship of the King and Queen of Spain, Columbus began his voyage from mainland Spain on August 3, 1492. He commanded three ships: the Niña, the Pinta, and the Santa Maria. On October 12, a sailor aboard the Pinta sighted an island in what is the present day Bahamas. Columbus named the island San Salvador. After exploring five islands in the Bahamas, Columbus reached Cuba on October 28. It was there that Columbus and his crew discovered the smoking of tobacco, a habit they quickly adopted. Leaving Cuba, Columbus made landfall on the Island of Hispaniola on December 5. He was fond of this island because it reminded him of Spain. He also found some gold there. On December 24 the Santa Maria ran aground and had to be abandoned. Columbus decided that it was time to return to Spain and set out with the two remaining ships on January 16, 1493. The ships reached Lisbon, Portugal on March 4, and on March 15 Columbus and his ships pulled into port in Spain.

Now, construct a series of events graphic organizer about this information on the blank page that follows.

Unit 7: Graphic Organizers and Charts

Activity 7-2: Series of Events Graphic Organizer (continued)

Construct your series of events graphic organizer here.

Unit 7: Graphic Organizers and Charts

Activity 7-3: Compare-Contrast Graphic Organizer

Activity 7-3: Compare-Contrast Graphic Organizer

A compare-contrast graphic organizer helps you to show how two things are both alike and different. Usually there are more ways in which two things are different than ways in which they are alike.

Read the following information about Democrats and Republicans.

> The Democratic Party and the Republican Party are the two major political parties in the United States. Each funds its campaigns through donations. While these parties have many differences in their social, economic, and military views, each party functions to provide political leadership, government, and policy formation. Broadly speaking, Democrats are known as liberals and Republicans as conservatives. Democrats typically support a broader range of social services than those advocated by Republicans. While Democrats lean toward an active role for government in society, Republicans favor a limited role. The differing philosophies of the two parties have resulted in opposite stands on a number of issues. While Democrats prefer decreased military spending, the opposite is true for Republicans. Taxes are a bone of contention. Republicans support the idea of tax cuts across the board, whereas Democrats would like to increase taxes on the wealthy. Given their support of business, Republicans are reluctant to raise the minimum wage because they believe it would hurt business. On the other hand, Democrats favor increasing the minimum wage to help workers. If you have watched television coverage of national elections, you probably know that the color Red has become associated with the Republicans and Blue with the Democrats. You probably can also immediately recognize the Democrat Party donkey logo versus the Republican Party elephant logo.

Unit 7: Graphic Organizers and Charts

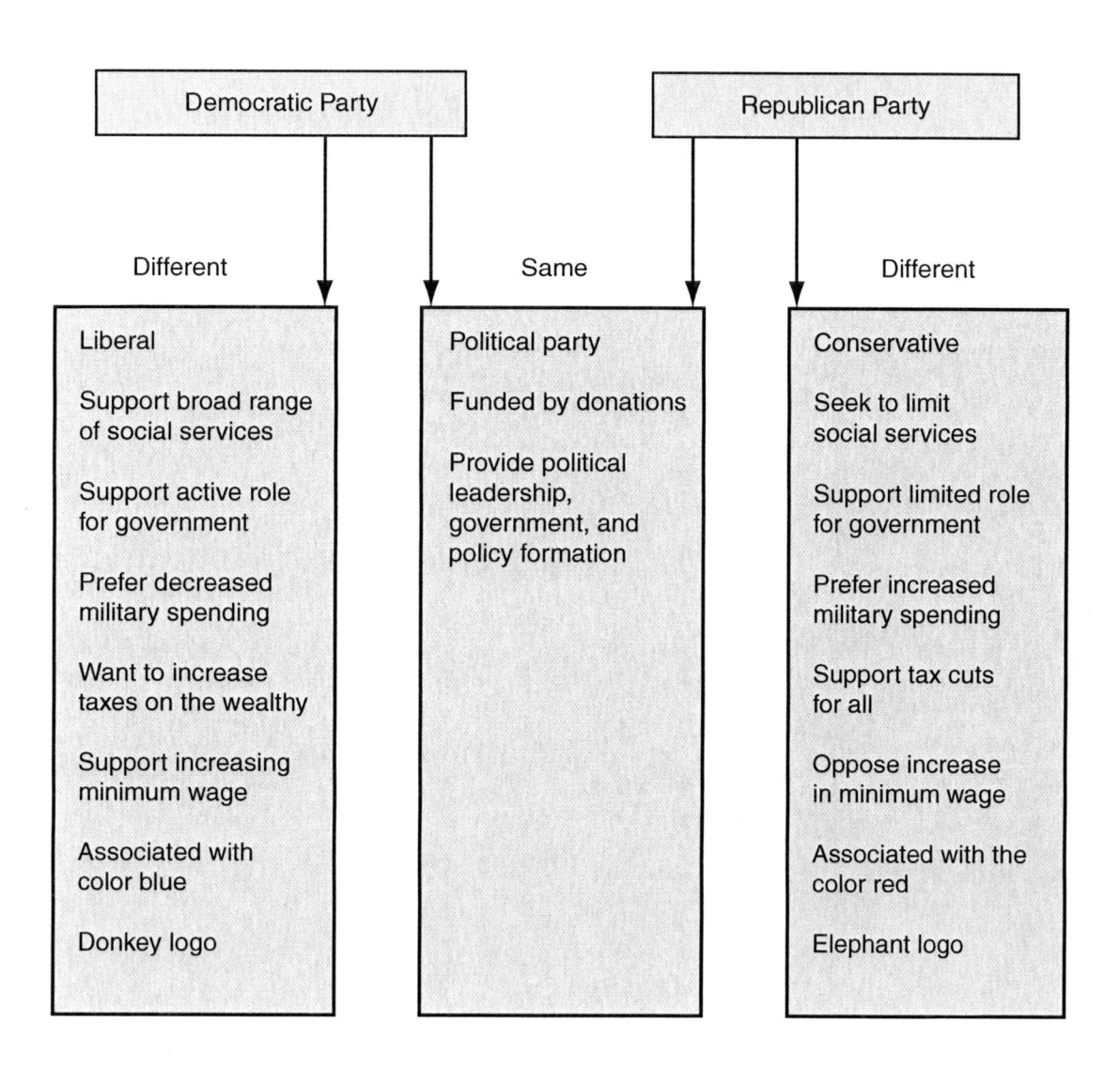

Activity 7-3: Compare-Contrast Graphic Organizer (continued)

Here is a compare-contrast graphic organizer a student constructed from the information presented about the Democratic and Republican Parties. This illustrates how a compare-contrast graphic organizer is constructed.

Democratic Party		Republican Party
Different	**Same**	**Different**
Liberal	Political party	Conservative
Support broad range of social services	Funded by donations	Seek to limit social services
Support active role for government	Provide political leadership, government, and policy formation	Support limited role for government
Prefer decreased military spending		Prefer increased military spending
Want to increase taxes on the wealthy		Support tax cuts for all
Support increasing minimum wage		Oppose increase in minimum wage
Associated with color blue		Associated with the color red
Donkey logo		Elephant logo

Unit 7: Graphic Organizers and Charts

Activity 7-3: Compare-Contrast Graphic Organizer (continued)

Read the following information about vertebrates and invertebrates.

> Animals can be classified into two main groups, vertebrates and invertebrates. The main difference between them is that invertebrates do not have a backbone or a spinal column. Both vertebrates and invertebrates belong to Kingdom Animalia and to the Chordata Phylum. There is an enormous difference regarding the number of species. There are approximately two million species of invertebrates, but less than sixty thousand species of vertebrates. Vertebrates are usually large in size, while invertebrates are usually small. Both types of animals can live in a variety of habitats. Vertebrates can move faster than can invertebrates. In contrast to invertebrates, vertebrates have a highly developed nervous system. This allows vertebrates to be more adaptable than invertebrates to changes in their surroundings.

Now, construct a compare-contrast graphic organizer about this information on the blank page that follows.

Unit 7: Graphic Organizers and Charts

Activity 7-3: Compare-Contrast Graphic Organizer (continued)

Construct your compare-contrast graphic organizer here.

Activity 7-4: Problem-Solution Graphic Organizer

A problem-solution graphic organizer allows you to understand a problem, attempts to reach a solution, and the current status of the problem.

Read the following information about the problem of acid rain.

> Acid rain is precipitation that has a high concentration of acid from pollutants such as sulfur dioxide and nitrogen oxide. It is a result of the burning of fossil fuels in industry and vehicles and the releasing of chemicals by certain industrial processes. Acid rain has destructive effects on plant and animal life. It also accelerates the decay of building materials and paints. There are a number of ways in which society has attempted to reduce and ultimately eliminate acid rain. The burning of coal is one of the major contributors to acid rain. There have been efforts to use coal that contains less sulfur. Other efforts are washing and scrubbing the coal so that less gas leaves a smokestack when the coal is burned. Some power plants have switched to alternative energy sources in place of coal. Nuclear power and hydropower are being used increasingly. Natural gas powered and battery powered cars are another way in which alternative energy sources are being used to deal with the problem of acid rain. Environmentally conscious individuals have helped by turning off lights and appliances when not in use, purchasing energy efficient appliances, insulating homes, and carpooling or using public transportation. All of these efforts have borne fruit. Although there is still progress to be made, a lot has been accomplished already, and the problem of acid rain is beginning to disappear.

On the next page is a problem-solution graphic organizer a student constructed from the information presented about the problem of acid rain. It illustrates how to construct a problem-solution graphic organizer.

Unit 7: Graphic Organizers and Charts

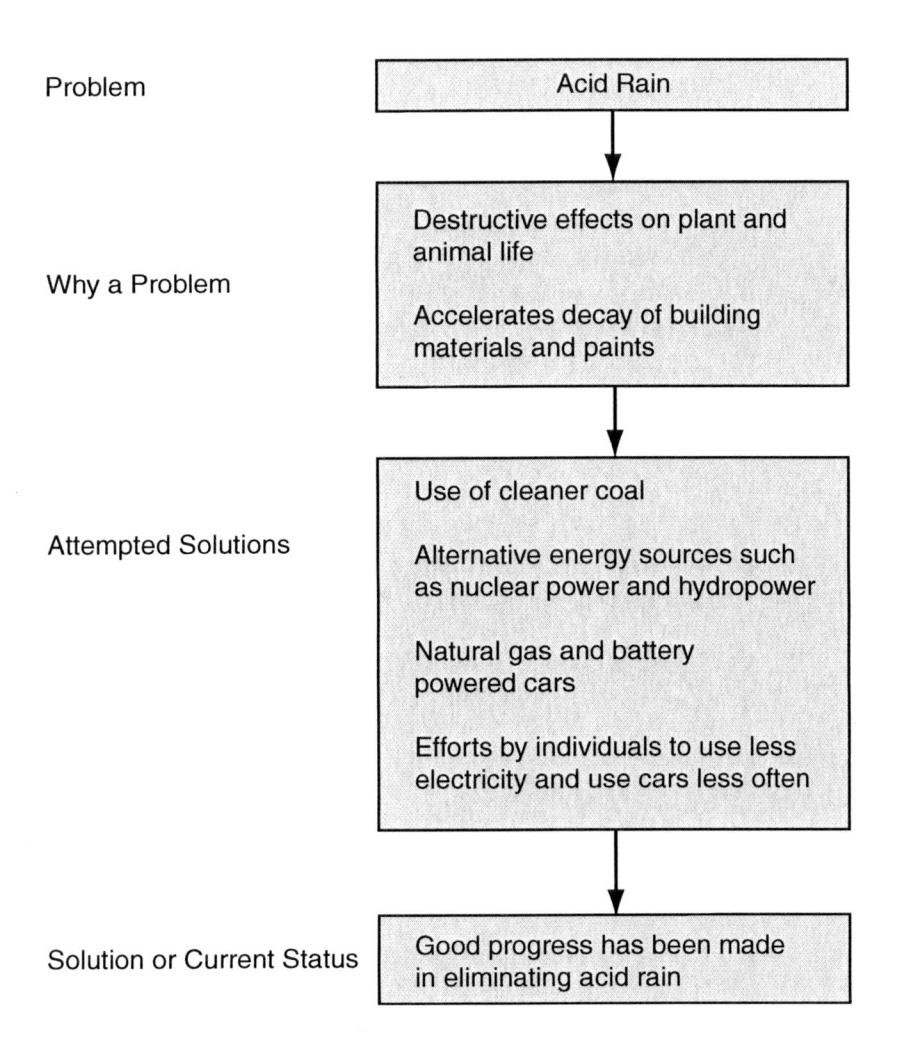

Activity 7-4: Problem-Solution Graphic Organizer (continued)

Problem	Acid Rain
Why a Problem	Destructive effects on plant and animal life Accelerates decay of building materials and paints
Attempted Solutions	Use of cleaner coal Alternative energy sources such as nuclear power and hydropower Natural gas and battery powered cars Efforts by individuals to use less electricity and use cars less often
Solution or Current Status	Good progress has been made in eliminating acid rain

Unit 7: Graphic Organizers and Charts

Activity 7-4: Problem-Solution Graphic Organizer (continued)

Read the following information about cancer.

> Cancer is a significant health problem. It is the second leading cause of death in the United States. Extensive research has gone into the quest for treatments that will minimize the effects of cancer and save the lives of many people. As a result, there are several promising treatments that are being used today. Chemotherapy is probably the most effective way to treat cancer. In chemotherapy, various medications are used to kill cancer cells. Another effective treatment is radiotherapy. This treatment uses radiation to destroy cancer cells. One of the newer treatment methods is the use of biological therapy. In this method, the body's immune system is used to help fight the cancer cells. Finally, although a highly controversial treatment, some specialists report success with the use of natural herbs such as garlic, chaparral, red clover, poke root, and echinacea. While cancer remains a major health problem in the United States, cancer death rates among both men and women are continuing to decline.

Now, construct a problem-solution graphic organizer about this information on the blank page that follows.

Construct your problem-solution graphic organizer here.

Unit 7: Graphic Organizers and Charts

Activity 7-5: Question-Answer Graphic Organizer

Activity 7-5: Question-Answer Graphic Organizer

A question-answer graphic organizer is a good tool to use when you have specific questions about a topic you are studying. It helps you to clearly identify your questions and to organize your answers to the questions.

Adam saw an old Model T Ford at an auto show. He was curious about when it was produced, how much it cost at the time it was produced, why it became so popular, and whether there were any problems with it. He read the following article from an Internet site to find answers to his questions.

> The Model T automobile was built by the Ford Motor Company from 1908 until 1927. Henry Ford wanted to develop a practical means of transportation that most people could afford. The Model T was the answer. It quickly became prized for its low cost, durability, versatility, and ease of maintenance. It was so dependable that it was nicknamed the "Tin Lizzie." "Lizzie" was a slang term at the time that was used to describe a reliable servant. Thanks to the assembly-line production of the Model T its prices remained low. In fact, the prices dropped from $850 in 1908 to less than $300 in 1925. No wonder the Model T accounted for almost 40 percent of all cars sold in the United States during its years of production. For most of its production years the car was available only in black. When asked about color choices, Ford was known to jokingly reply that buyers could choose any color as long as it was black. The Model T's four cylinder engine generated 20 horsepower and allowed the car to reach speeds as high as 45 miles per hour. The Model T was not without its problems. The ride was bumpy, particularly at its higher speeds, and the car's incessant rattles rattled people's nerves (forgive the pun). Further, many people regarded the car, to put it mildly, as ugly.

After Adam read the article about the Model T, he constructed the question-answer graphic organizer shown on the next page. It illustrates how to create a question-answer graphic organizer.

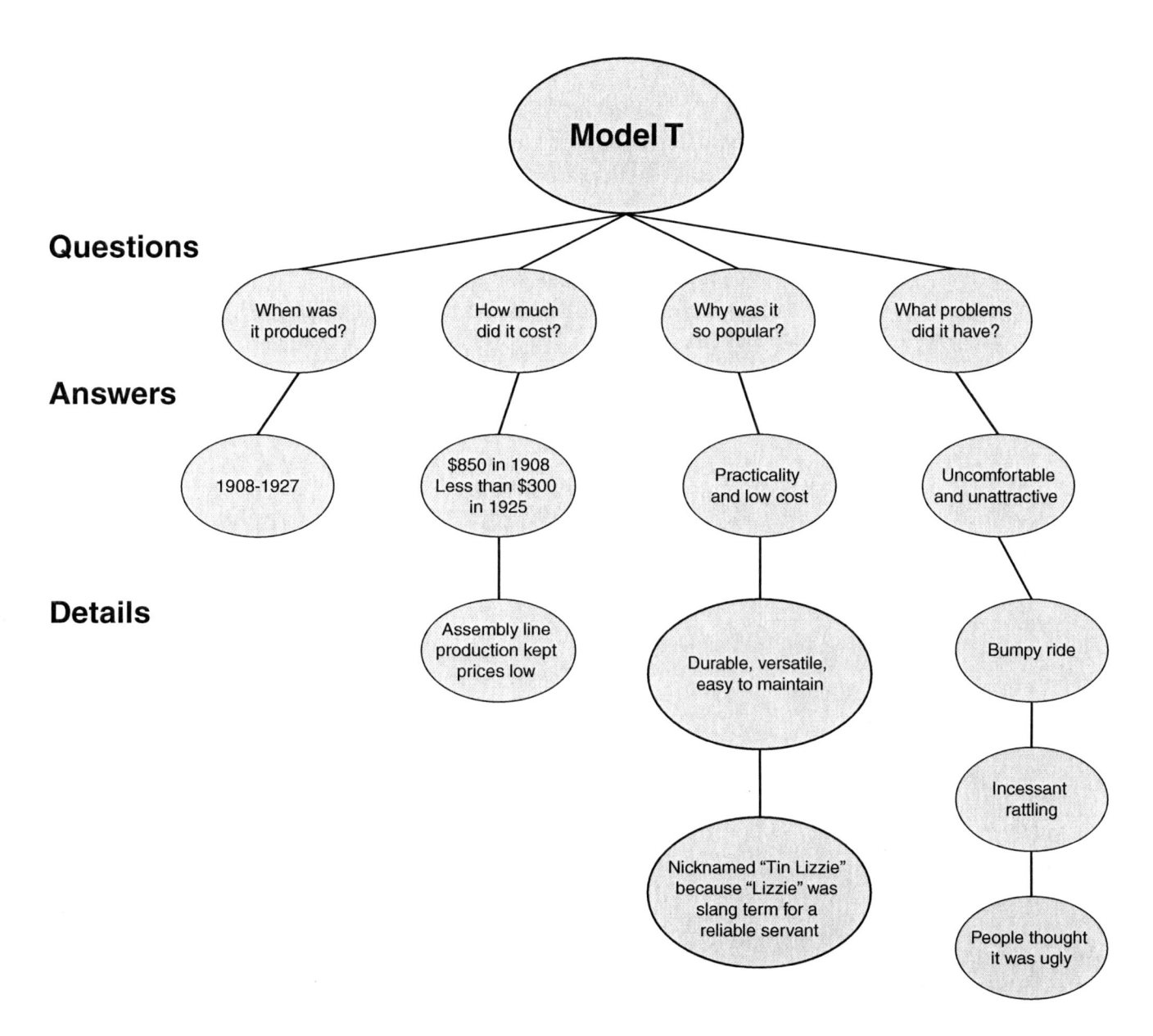

Unit 7: Graphic Organizers and Charts

Activity 7-5: Question-Answer Graphic Organizer (continued)

Model T

Questions

- When was it produced?
- How much did it cost?
- Why was it so popular?
- What problems did it have?

Answers

- 1908-1927
- $850 in 1908 Less than $300 in 1925
- Practicality and low cost
- Uncomfortable and unattractive

Details

- Assembly line production kept prices low
- Durable, versatile, easy to maintain
  - Nicknamed "Tin Lizzie" because "Lizzie" was slang term for a reliable servant
- Bumpy ride
  - Incessant rattling
  - People thought it was ugly

Unit 7: Graphic Organizers and Charts

Activity 7-5: Question-Answer Graphic Organizer (continued)

Janice briefly heard about the Sacco-Vanzetti case in her sociology class. She knew that it was a famous murder trial that took place sometime in the 1920s. She was curious about who Sacco and Vanzetti were and exactly what they were tried for. Janice wasn't sure exactly when the trial took place. Her teacher had mentioned that there were some issues surrounding the case but had not gone further. Janice also wanted to know what the issues were. She found an article on the Internet that helped her learn more about the case.

Read the following article that Janice found about the Sacco-Vanzetti trial.

> On April 15, 1920 in South Braintree, Massachusetts, a paymaster and a security guard for a shoe company were delivering a payroll for the business. The paymaster and guard were shot and killed by two men who stole the payroll and fled by automobile. On May 5, Nicola Sacco and Bartolomeo Vanzetti were arrested and charged with the murders and robbery. Both were Italian immigrants who had come to the United States in 1908. Sacco worked as a shoemaker while Vanzetti worked as a fish peddler. The two were political anarchists who opposed all governments. Their opposition to World War I led them to emigrate from the United States to Mexico to avoid the army draft. They returned to the United States in 1920, where they settled in Massachusetts. Sacco and Vanzetti were brought to trial on May 13, 1921, and were found guilty on both charges on July 14, 1921. The verdict generated a storm of protest throughout the nation. Many people felt that the trial had been less than fair in that the defendants had been convicted for their radical, anarchist beliefs rather than for the crimes for which they were charged. Critics also pointed out that Sacco and Vanzetti knew very little English; consequently, they gave confusing and false answers during their interrogation which diminished their credibility with the jury. Many felt that the police evidence against Sacco and Vanzetti was weak. Sacco owned a pistol of the type used in the murders, and the men had been arrested at a garage where they were attempting to reclaim a damaged automobile that had been seen in the vicinity of the crime. Over the next six years, their lawyers presented many motions asking for a new trial. These motions were to no avail, and Sacco and Vanzetti were executed on August 23, 1927. Their guilt or innocence continues to be debated to this day.

Now, construct a question-answer graphic organizer about this information on the blank page that follows.

Unit 7: Graphic Organizers and Charts

Activity 7-5: Question-Answer Graphic Organizer (continued)

Construct your question-answer graphic organizer here.

Unit 7: Graphic Organizers and Charts

Activity 7-6: Cause-Effect Graphic Organizer

Activity 7-6: Cause-Effect Graphic Organizer

A **cause-effect graphic organizer** shows how something can have a number of effects. The effects can be positive, negative, or both.

Read the following information about Hurricane Katrina.

> Hurricane Katrina struck the southeastern Gulf Coast of the United States on August 29, 2005. It made landfall approximately 45 miles southeast of New Orleans as a category 4 hurricane. The effects of this hurricane were significant in a number of ways. There were a number of economic consequences. The overall economic impact of Hurricane Katrina was estimated to be 150 billion dollars. This made it the costliest natural disaster in the history of the United States. The factor that contributed to this cost was a drop in oil production, food exports, and other forms of trade and business. Further, tourism fell off sharply. The effects on the environment were considerable. Industrial wastes, oil spills, sewage, toxic chemicals, and other hazardous pollutants hit the area of impact and surrounding areas, while contaminated floodwater overflowed into residential areas. The result was short-term and long-term health problems for humans and animals. The social effects of Katrina are sometimes overlooked, but they were considerable in their own right. More than 1,800 people lost their lives in this disaster. Many people lost their homes and jobs. Understandably, these losses were associated with considerable emotional and psychological stress.

On the next page is a cause-effect graphic organizer a student constructed about Hurricane Katrina. It illustrates how a cause-effect graphic organizer is constructed.

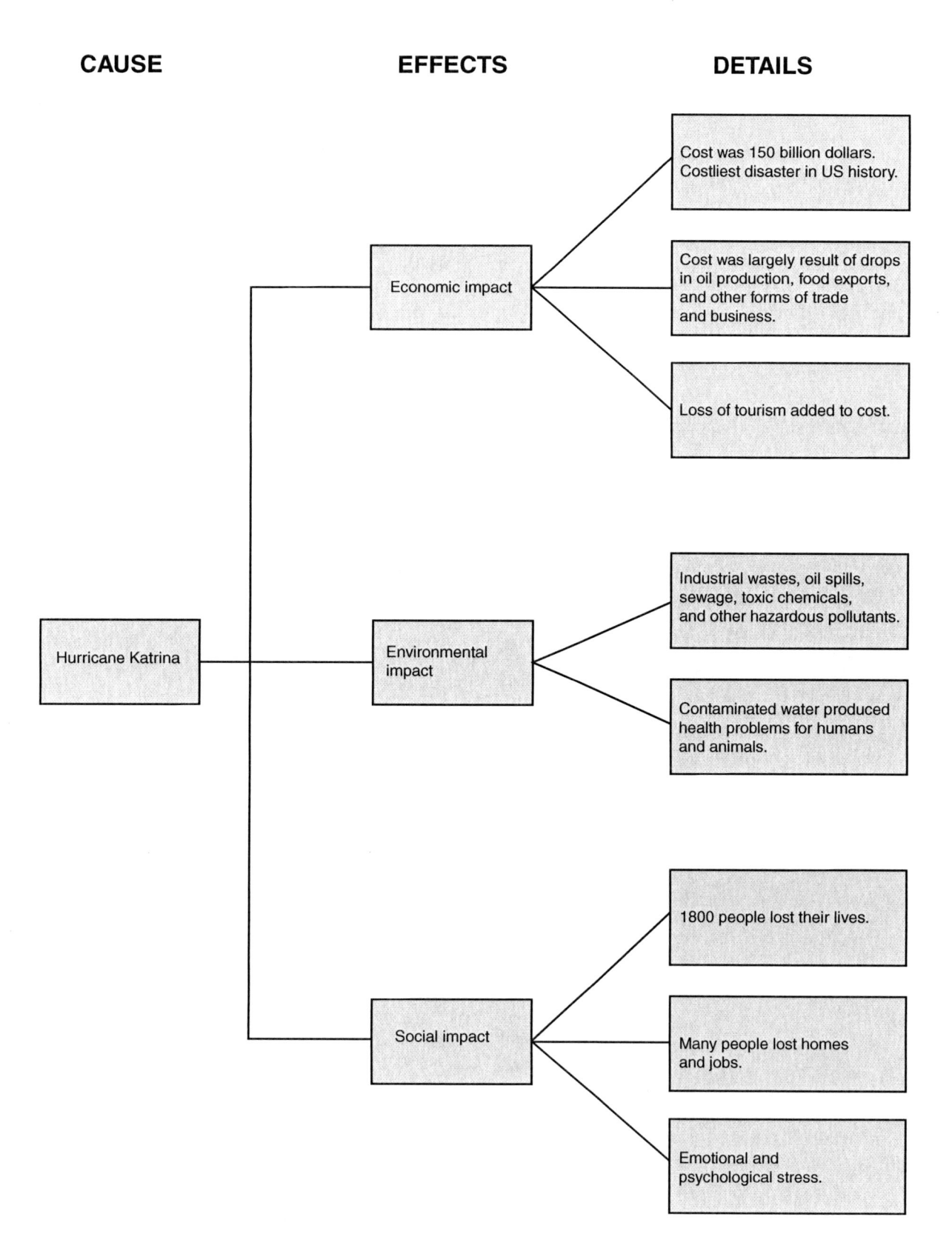

Unit 7: Graphic Organizers and Charts

Activity 7-6: Cause-Effect Graphic Organizer (continued)

CAUSE   **EFFECTS**   **DETAILS**

Hurricane Katrina

- **Economic impact**
  - Cost was 150 billion dollars. Costliest disaster in US history.
  - Cost was largely result of drops in oil production, food exports, and other forms of trade and business.
  - Loss of tourism added to cost.

- **Environmental impact**
  - Industrial wastes, oil spills, sewage, toxic chemicals, and other hazardous pollutants.
  - Contaminated water produced health problems for humans and animals.

- **Social impact**
  - 1800 people lost their lives.
  - Many people lost homes and jobs.
  - Emotional and psychological stress.

Unit 7: Graphic Organizers and Charts

Activity 7-6: Cause-Effect Graphic Organizer (continued)

Read the following article about the depletion of the ozone layer.

> The ozone layer is a belt of naturally occurring ozone gas that sits about 15 to 30 kilometers above Earth. It serves as a shield from the harmful ultraviolet B radiation emitted by the sun. Today, there is widespread concern that the ozone layer is deteriorating due to the release of pollution containing the chemicals chlorine and bromine. Chlorofluorocarbons (CFCs), chemicals found in spray aerosols, are a major factor in the depletion of the ozone layer. The depletion of the ozone layer is linked to increased cancer levels, especially skin cancers. An increase in malaria and other infectious diseases has been noted. Adverse effects on the eyes have been reported. These include the afflictions of pterygium and keratopathy. Both of these afflictions can reduce clarity of vision and even result in blindness. An increase in cataracts that cloud the lens of the eye has also been widely reported. There is concern that the life cycles of plants will change, adversely affecting the food chain. Unusual plant growth patterns have been found in some parts of the world, with some plants stunted, and others showing enhanced growth. Even the oceans have been affected, with the reproductive cycle of phytoplankton being inhibited. Since phytoplankton, such as algae, are organisms that are at the bottom of the food chain, the population of fish and other ocean animals faces reduction.

Now, construct a cause-effect graphic organizer about this information on the blank page that follows.

Unit 7: Graphic Organizers and Charts

Activity 7-6: Cause-Effect Graphic Organizer (continued)

Construct your cause-effect graphic organizer here.

Activity 7-7: Series of Steps Chart

A **series of steps** chart shows the steps to follow to accomplish something. The steps are shown in the order in which they should be performed.

Read the following information about how to make a clay pottery bowl.

> To make a clay pottery bowl, begin by softening enough clay to make the bowl by working the clay with your fingers and pounding on it. Then form the softened clay into an upside down cone shape. Place the cone-shaped clay on a pottery wheel, wet your hands, and lightly wet the clay. Push the clay down as the wheel is spinning to flatten the clay's peak. Then cup your hands on the sides to shape the bottom of the bowl and continue to push the clay down so that its top is flat. Make a hole at the center of the clay by slowly and lightly pushing your thumbs into the clay and keep pinching the clay with your fingers to widen the hole. Turn off the pottery wheel, remove the bowl, and bring it to a pottery shop that has a kiln in which your bowl can be hardened and finished.

On the following page is a sequence chart a student constructed about the steps to follow when making a clay pottery bowl. It illustrates how a series of steps chart is constructed.

Unit 7: Graphic Organizers and Charts

Activity 7-7: Series of Steps Chart (continued)

Thing to be Accomplished	Make a clay pottery bowl.
First	Soften enough clay to make the bowl by working the clay with your fingers and pounding on it.
Next	Form the softened clay into an upside down cone shape.
Next	Place the cone shaped clay on a pottery wheel.
Next	Wet your hands and the clay and push the clay down as the wheel is spinning to flatten the clay's peak.
Next	Slowly and lightly push your thumbs into the clay to make a hole at its center.
Next	Keep pinching the clay until the hole is wide enough.
Last	Remove the bowl from the wheel and take it to a pottery shop where it can be hardened and finished in a kiln.

Unit 7: Graphic Organizers and Charts

Activity 7-7: Series of Steps Chart (continued)

Read the following article about writing a research paper.

> The first thing to do to write a good research paper is to choose a topic that you find interesting. There should be enough information to allow you write a paper about the topic. Locate the information you need to write your paper by using print and online reference sources. Prepare a bibliography card each time you find a source that you will use. Use note cards to record notes from each source. It is a good idea to number your note cards so that you can keep track of your information. When you have sufficient information, prepare an outline of your notes. Your outline should include subtopics and details about your topic. Now you are ready to write a rough draft of your paper. Review your rough draft to check for errors and to see how you can improve your paper. At last you are ready to write your final paper.

Now, use the information in the article to construct a series of steps chart that shows how to write a good research paper on the blank page that follows.

Unit 7: Graphic Organizers and Charts
Activity 7-7: Series of Steps Chart (continued)

Construct your series of steps chart here.

Activity 7-8: Five W's Chart

Writers are trained to include information about <u>w</u>ho, <u>w</u>hat, <u>w</u>here, <u>w</u>hen, and <u>w</u>hy when they write articles for newspapers and magazines. A **five W's** chart can help you to organize and understand the information found in newspaper and magazine articles. Sometimes, one or more of the five W's may not be included in an article.

Read the following abridged newspaper article from the New York Times of October 14, 1964.

> Oslo, Norway, Oct. 14 — The Nobel Peace Prize for 1964 was awarded today to the Rev. Dr. Martin Luther King Jr. The 35-year-old civil rights leader is the youngest winner of the prize since the first was awarded in 1901. The prize honors acts "for the furtherance of brotherhood among men..." Dr. King said that "every penny" of the prize money, which amounts to about $54,000, will be given to the civil rights movement. He also said he saw no political implications in the award. Dr. King is the twelfth American to be awarded the peace prize. The award to Dr. King will be made in Oslo Dec. 10.

Here is a five W's chart a student constructed from the article about Dr. King's award. This illustrates how a five W's chart is constructed.

Who was involved?	Martin Luther King Jr.
What happened?	Dr. King was awarded the Nobel Peace prize.
Where did it take place?	Oslo, Norway
When did it take place?	October 14, 1964
Why did it happen?	Dr. King was awarded the prize for his furtherance of brotherhood among men.

Unit 7: Graphic Organizers and Charts

Activity 7-8: Five W's Chart (continued)

Read the following abridged newspaper article from the New York Times of October 17, 1931.

> Chicago, Oct. 17 — Al Capone was found guilty here tonight on five of the twenty-three counts contained in the two indictments brought against him by the Federal Government for income tax evasion from 1924 to 1929. Two of the five counts are misdemeanors… the other counts on which he was found guilty are felonies…
> The verdict, returned eight hours and ten minutes after the jury filed out at 2:40 P.M., was a puzzling one to all in the court room. Capone grinned as though he felt he had gotten off easily. Capone faces a maximum sentence of seventeen years' imprisonment and a $50,000 fine. He did not seem to realize that. As soon as the verdict was entered, he got out of his seat and virtually ran from the room. The Capone trial started on Oct. 6 after the government had spent three years preparing for it.

Now, use the information in the article to construct a five W's chart on the blank page that follows.

Unit 7: Graphic Organizers and Charts
Activity 7-8: Five W's Chart (continued)

Construct your five W's chart here.

Activity 7-9: KWL Chart

A **KWL chart** is a useful tool when you want to learn more about a topic.

K represents what you already **know** about the topic.

W represents what else you **want** to know about the topic.

L represents what you **learn** about the topic.

A KWL chart consists of three columns, one for each of the three letters. Kevin was learning about famous early Americans in his history class. He wanted to know more about Benjamin Franklin. To use the KWL chart, Kevin completed the first two columns as follows. He left enough space between each question he wrote in the W column so that each answer in the L column would be next to its question.

Topic: Benjamin Franklin		
K	**W**	**L**
Franklin was an inventor.	What did he invent?	
He lived in the 1700's.		
He wrote many things.	What things did he write?	
	What made him famous?	
	What else did he do?	

Kevin then read the following article about Benjamin Franklin.

> Benjamin Franklin was one of the most important and famous people of the 18th century. Most Europeans in the first half of the 18th century thought of America as a primitive and undeveloped country. Franklin's discoveries about electricity in the middle of the century changed their perceptions. His contributions to the science of electricity surpassed those of Europe's greatest scientific minds. But more important to Franklin was what he could do in the service of his country. It turned out that he could do a great deal. During the American Revolutionary War, Franklin secured financial and military aid from France that was instrumental in the colonists' struggle for independence from England. His diplomatic skills and accomplishments were unparalleled. Franklin contributed to the writing of both the Declaration of Independence and the Constitution. Franklin's contributions to the comfort and safety of daily life were numerous and significant. His invention of the lightning rod spared many homes all over the world from destruction, as well as saving many lives. Franklin invented a wood-burning stove that is still in use today. He invented bifocal glasses, the odometer, and even a musical instrument known as an armonica. In his adopted home city of Philadelphia, he was instrumental in the establishment of institutions such as fire companies, libraries, insurance companies, academies, hospitals, and civic societies. He certainly took to heart one of the maxims he published in *Poor Richard's Almanac*: "Early to bed, early to rise, makes a man healthy, wealthy, and wise."

Unit 7: Graphic Organizers and Charts

Activity 7-9: KWL Chart (continued)

As he read the article, Kevin completed the KWL chart. Here is his completed chart.

Topic: Benjamin Franklin		
K	**W**	**L**
Franklin was an inventor.	What did he invent?	He invented the lightning rod, wood-burning stove, bifocals, odometer, and armonica.
He lived in the 1700's.		Philadelphia was his adopted home city.
He wrote many things.	What things did he write?	He contributed to the writing of the Declaration of Independence and the Constitution. He wrote "Poor Richard's Almanac."
	What made him famous?	His work related to electricity surpassed that of the European scientists, and brought him fame across the world.
	What else did he do?	He was a diplomat to France during the Revolutionary War and secured their financial and military aid in the fight against England.
		He helped to establish institutions such as fire companies, libraries, insurance companies, academies, hospitals, and civic societies.

Unit 7: Graphic Organizers and Charts

Activity 7-9: KWL Chart (continued)

Choose a topic you want to learn more about. Construct a KWL chart for this topic here.

Unit 7: Graphic Organizers and Charts

Activity 7-10: What I Have Learned

Activity 7-10: What I Have Learned

Here are the names of the graphic organizers and charts you have learned about in this unit.

Cause-Effect Graphic Organizer

Compare-Contrast Graphic Organizer

Five W's Chart

KWL Chart

Problem-Solution Graphic Organizer

Question-Answer Graphic Organizer

Series of Steps Chart

Series of Events Graphic Organizer

Topic-List Graphic Organizer

For each of the following, write the name of the graphic organizer or chart that would be best to use. Use each graphic organizer or chart just once.

1. You are concerned about the problem of world poverty. You read an article about what we can do to reduce world poverty.

   _____

2. You are learning about plant and animal cells in your biology class. You want to show how these cells are similar in some ways and different in other ways.

   _____

3. You read an article about how obesity results in many health and social problems.

   _____

4. You read an article in your local newspaper about the mayor's plans to renovate the downtown area.

   _____

5. You know some things about our galaxy, but you want to learn more about it.

   _____

Unit 7: Graphic Organizers and Charts

Activity 7-10: What I Have Learned (continued)

6. You read a very detailed article about the Great Depression. You want to organize the information showing subtopics and details.

   _____

7. You have read several articles to help you answer some questions you have about the Electoral College.

   _____

8. You are studying the events that led to the Boston Tea Party.

   _____

9. You read a blog about how to make your own ice cream

   _____

Unit 8
Taking Tests

Activities

8-1   The DETER Test Taking Strategy

8-2   Learning About Multiple-Choice Tests

8-3   Doing Well on Multiple-Choice Tests

8-4   Doing Well on True/False Tests

8-5   Demonstrating Mastery of True/False Tests

8-6   Learning About Matching Tests

8-7   Doing Well on Matching Tests

8-8   Learning About Completion Tests

8-9   Guidelines for Taking Completion Tests

8-10 Learning About Essay Tests

8-11 Direction Words in Essay Test Items

8-12 Practice Writing a Response to an Essay Test Item

8-13 Reviewing Your Response to an Essay Test Item

8-14 What I Have Learned

Unit 8: Taking Tests

Activity 8-1: The DETER Test Taking Strategy

Activity 8-1: The DETER Test Taking Strategy

You will be learning about five types of tests in this unit: multiple-choice, true/false, matching, completion, and essay. **DETER** is a strategy that will help you to do your best when you take each of these types of tests. Each letter in DETER stands for a step in the strategy. Read the following information to learn what to do for each step in DETER.

D Read the test **Directions** carefully. Be sure that you know what you have to do to complete the test. Ask your teacher to explain anything about the directions you do not understand.

E Examine the entire test to see how much there is to do. This will help you to establish a mental set for taking the test.

T Plan how much **Time** to spend answering each item. You can do this by dividing the number of minutes you have to take the test by the number of items. If all of the items do not count for the same number of points, plan to spend more time on those items that count for the most points.

E Answer the items you find **Easiest** first. By doing this, you will be able to answer the questions you are sure about before time runs out.

R Review your answers to be sure they are your best answers. Be sure that you have answered all required items.

Answer the following questions.

1. What does the second **E** stand for in the DETER strategy?

   _____

2. What can examining all the test items before answering the items help you to do?

   _____

3. Why should you answer the items you find easiest first?

   _____

4. If all items count for the same number of points, what is a good way to determine how much time you should spend answering each item?

   _____

Unit 8: Taking Tests

Activity 8-2: Learning About Multiple-Choice Tests

Activity 8-2: Learning About Multiple-Choice Tests

A **multiple-choice** test contains items that consist of a stem (a question or an incomplete statement) and several *answer choices* from which you are to choose the correct choice. Typically there are four answer choices that are represented by the letters a, b, c, and d, or as (1), (2), (3), and (4).

Look at the following example of an item in which the stem is presented as a question. You should select "a" as the answer choice that correctly answers the question.

> Which one of the following was a result of the Industrial Revolution in Europe?
> a. The growth of the middle class.
> b. An increase of nomadic herding.
> c. A decline in urban population.
> d. A decrease in international trade.

Here is an example of the same item with the stem presented as an incomplete statement. In this form, the missing part of the statement can appear anywhere in the statement. You should select "a" as the answer choice that correctly completes the statement.

> _____ was a result of the Industrial Revolution in Europe.
> a. The growth of the middle class
> b. An increase of nomadic herding
> c. A decline in urban population
> d. A decrease in international trade

Unit 8: Taking Tests

Activity 8-2: Learning About Multiple-Choice Tests (continued)

Sometimes you will find more than one missing part in a statement. Here is an example for which (3) is the correct answer choice.

If there is nothing to absorb the energy of sound waves, they travel on _____, but their intensity _____ as they travel further from their source.

(1) erratically - mitigates

(2) eternally - alleviates

(3) indefinitely - diminishes

(4) forever - increases

(5) steadily - stabilizes

Sometimes, one of the answer choices in a multiple-choice item is "all of the above." Look at the following example. In this example, "all of the above" is the correct answer choice because all of the countries shown as answer choices are in South America.

Which of the following countries is in South America?

a. Bolivia

b. Uruguay

c. Argentina

d. Ecuador

e. all of the above

Unit 8: Taking Tests

Activity 8-2: Learning About Multiple-Choice Tests (continued)

Other times, one of the answer choices is "none of the above." Look at the following example. In this example, "none of the above" is *not* the correct answer choice because Italy is in Europe. For "none of the above" to be the correct answer choice, none of the countries shown as answer choices could be in Europe. The correct answer choice in this case is (3).

_____ is a country in Europe.

(1) Bolivia

(2) Uruguay

(3) Italy

(4) Ecuador

(5) none of the above

Use the information in the box that follows to write two multiple-choice test items. Your first item should be an incomplete statement followed by four answer choices. Your second item should be a question followed by four answer choices.

Year: 1876

Event: Alexander Graham Bell invented the telephone

---

1. _____

   a. _____

   b. _____

   c. _____

   d. _____

Unit 8: Taking Tests

Activity 8-2: Learning About Multiple-Choice Tests (continued)

2. _____

    a. _____

    b. _____

    c. _____

    d. _____

Now, use the information in the box that follows to write a multiple-choice item for which one of the answer choices is "all of the above." When writing the item, "all of the above" does not have to be the correct answer choice.

> Bears, skunks, chickens, turtles, and piranhas are carnivores. Cows, elephants, iguanas, fruit bats, and manatees are herbivores.

3. _____

    (1) _____

    (2) _____

    (3) _____

    (4) _____

    (5) _____

Unit 8: Taking Tests

Activity 8-2: Learning About Multiple-Choice Tests (continued)

This time, use the information in the box that follows to write a multiple-choice item for which one of the answer choices is "none of the above." When writing the item, "none of the above" does not have to be the correct answer choice.

> The United States, England, Canada, Mexico, and India were part of the Allied Forces during World War II. Germany, Japan, Italy, Hungary, and Romania were members of the Axis Powers during this war.

4. _____

   a. _____

   b. _____

   c. _____

   d. _____

   e. _____

5. **Now, write some information from one of your textbooks or your class notes that you can use to create a multiple-choice item. Write the information here.**

_____

_____

_____

_____

6. **Now, write a multiple-choice item that is based on the information you just wrote.**

   a. _____

   b. _____

   c. _____

   d. _____

   e. _____

Unit 8: Taking Tests

Activity 8-3: Doing Well on Multiple-Choice Tests

Activity 8-3: Doing Well on Multiple-Choice Tests

Here are some guidelines that will help you to do your best when taking a multiple-choice test. Read these guidelines. Use them when you take the practice multiple-choice test that appears later in this activity and whenever you take a multiple-choice test.

- **Carefully read the test directions.** Usually you are asked to choose the *correct* answer choice. But sometimes you are asked to choose the *best* answer choice. When asked to choose the correct answer choice, there is only one choice that is correct. When asked to choose the best answer choice, there may be more than one answer choice that could be considered correct; you must select the choice that is better than the others.

- **Circle or underline important words in the statement or question.** Doing this will help you to make certain that you have read the statement or question carefully. This will help you to focus on the information needed to identify the correct answer choice.

- **Read all of the answer choices before selecting one as the correct choice.** Do not simply select the first answer choice that appears to be correct. One of the answer choices that follows might be the correct answer choice. The same guideline holds true when you are to select the best answer choice. The first correct choice you come to may not be the best one.

- **Cross out any answer choices that you are certain are incorrect.** Each incorrect answer choice is a distracter from the correct choice. Crossing out answer choices that you are certain are not correct will eliminate them as distracters and will help you to zero in on the correct choice.

- **Look for answer choices that contain absolute terms such as *all*, *always*, *never*, and *none*.** Answer choices that contain absolute terms are usually incorrect because there are almost always exceptions to anything. Answer choices that contain qualifiers such as *often*, *usually*, and *in certain cases* are more likely to be the correct choice.

- **Look for two answer choices that are opposites.** When two of the answer choices are opposites, one of them is likely to be the correct choice.

- **When answering an item, look for hints about the correct answer choice in other items on the test.** Sometimes the correct answer choice for an item is contained in the stem of another item on the test.

- **Look for answer choices that contain language used by your teacher or found in your textbook.** An answer choice that contains such language is often the correct choice.

Unit 8: Taking Tests

Activity 8-3: Doing Well on Multiple-Choice Tests (continued)

- **Look for grammatical clues.** For example, if the stem of an item ends with the indefinite article *an*, the correct or best answer choice probably begins with a vowel. Also look for subject-verb agreement clues.

- **Look for verbal associations between the stem and an answer choice.** An answer choice that includes key words or terms that are part of the stem is often the correct choice.

- **Select "all of the above" as an answer choice only if you are certain that all of the other answer choices are correct.** If even one of the other answer choices is incorrect, "all of the above" is not the correct answer choice. As a rule of thumb, if you are certain that at least two of the other answer choices are correct, "all of the above" is likely to be the correct answer choice.

- **Select "none of the above" as an answer choice only if you are certain that all of the other answer choices are incorrect.** If even just one of the other answer choices is correct, "none of the above" is not the correct answer choice.

- **Do not change your answer unless you become certain that a different answer choice is correct.** More often than not, your first choice is the correct answer choice. Research suggests that when students change their answer choice, they usually change from the correct choice to an incorrect choice.

- **Do not look for a pattern of correct answer choices based on the order in which the answer choices are presented.** The order of correct answer choices within items is usually random.

- **When the answer choices are numbers, choose one that is in the middle of the numerical range.** Answer choices that are at the upper or lower extreme of the range are usually incorrect.

- **Answer all items unless there is a penalty for incorrect answers.** If there is a penalty for incorrect answers, then answer only the questions for which you are certain about the answer. Guessing may not be beneficial to you. If there is no penalty for incorrect answers and you cannot make even an educated guess as to the correct answer choice, go with "b" or "c". Research has shown these to be the correct answer choice more often than are "a" or "d."

Unit 8: Taking Tests

Activity 8-3: Doing Well on Multiple-Choice Tests (continued)

Take the following multiple-choice test. This test is based on the guidelines for taking multiple-choice tests that you just read about in this activity.

Directions: Circle the letter in front of the answer choice you believe is correct. There is no penalty for incorrect answers.

1. When should you select an answer choice as the correct answer choice?

    a. After you have reread the statement or question.

    b. As soon as you come to what you think is the correct answer choice.

    c. After you have crossed out one answer choice.

    d. After you have read all of the answer choices.

2. Choose "all of the above" as the correct answer choice when _____

    a. all of the other answer choices are correct.

    b. some of the other answer choices are correct.

    c. most of the other answer choices are incorrect.

    d. none of the other answer choices are correct.

3. You should _____ an answer choice when you decide it is not the correct choice.

    a. choose

    b. cross out

    c. reread

    d. rewrite

4. Change your answer choice only when you are sure a different answer choice is _____

    a. shorter.

    b. correct.

    c. longer.

    d. incorrect.

Unit 8: Taking Tests

Activity 8-3: Doing Well on Multiple-Choice Tests (continued)

5. Which type of term in an answer choice usually means that the choice is incorrect?

   a. A confusing term.

   b. A scientific term.

   c. A mathematical term.

   d. An absolute term.

   e. None of the above.

6. Sometimes you can find a hint about the correct answer choice by _____

   a. counting the number of words in the stem.

   b. counting the number of words in each answer choice.

   c. looking at your answer choices for other items.

   d. looking at other items on the test.

7. An answer choice is likely to be correct if it contains _____

   a. words found in popular magazines.

   b. information from a newspaper.

   c. language used in your textbook.

   d. words you do not understand.

8. When should you answer all items?

   a. When you don't understand some of the items.

   b. When you are running out of time.

   c. When there is no penalty for incorrect answers.

   d. When there is a penalty for incorrect answers.

Unit 8: Taking Tests

Activity 8-3: Doing Well on Multiple-Choice Tests (continued)

9. Choose "none of the above" as the correct answer choice when _____

    a. all of the other answer choices are correct.

    b. some of the other answer choices are correct.

    c. none of the other answer choices are correct.

    d. most of the other answer choices are incorrect.

10. When two answer choices are _____ , one of them is usually correct.

    a. easy

    b. opposites

    c. difficult

    d. short

11. When there is no penalty for incorrect answers and you have no idea as to which choice is correct, choose ___ or ___ .

    a. a or c.

    b. b or c.

    3. a or d.

    4. b or d.

Score your test as your teacher goes over the answers with you. Your score for the test is your number correct. Enter your score in the box below to see how well you did.

My Score _____
10-11 = Excellent
8-9 = Good
0-7 = Review the guidelines presented in this activity

Unit 8: Taking Tests

Activity 8-4: Doing Well on True/False Tests

Activity 8-4: Doing Well on True/False Tests

Items on a **true/false** test require you to read a statement and then decide if the statement is *true* or *false*. True/false test items seem easy since you have a 50/50 chance of guessing the correct answer. However, true/false test items can be difficult because they test for very specific knowledge.

Here are some guidelines that can help you to do your best when taking a true/false test. Read these guidelines and use them when you take the practice true/false test later in this activity and whenever you take a true/false test.

- **Try to prove each statement false.** It is easier to prove that a statement is false than to prove that it is true. Select *false* if any part of the statement is false.

  Read this next statement. The statement is false because although coal is made up of carbon, tar, and oils, it is not made up of salt.

  Coal is a fossil fuel that is made up of carbon, tar, oils, and salt.

  If all parts of the statement are true, select *true*. Read the following statement. The statement is true because all four of these musical instruments are percussion instruments.

  Drums, bells, cymbals, and gongs are percussion instruments.

- **Carefully reread statements that contain a negative word such as *not* or a word that begins with a negative prefix such as *unreliable*.** Negative words such as *not* or negative prefixes such as *un* completely change the meaning of a statement.

  For example, the following two statements look very similar, yet the first statement is true while the negative word *not* makes the second statement false.

  Green plants are the only plants that produce oxygen and make their own food.

  Green plants are not the only plants that produce oxygen and make their own food.

  In the following two statements, the second statement is *false* because of the prefix "dis" that begins the word "distrust."

  You should trust an honest man.

  You should distrust an honest man.

Unit 8: Taking Tests

Activity 8-4: Doing Well on True/False Tests (continued)

- **If a statement has two negatives, cross out both negatives.** Two negatives make a positive, but in a confusing way. Crossing out the two negatives will make it easier for you to understand the meaning of the statement. Read the two statements that follow. The second statement is easier to understand as true because the negatives *not* and *do not* have been crossed out.

    You will not succeed in life if you do not apply yourself.

    You will ~~not~~ succeed in life if you ~~do not~~ apply yourself.

- **Absolute statements are usually false. Qualified statements are usually true.** Absolute statements include words such as *all, none, always,* and *every.* Qualified statements include words such as *some, many, usually,* and *most.*

    Read the following two statements. The absolute word *all* in the first statement makes the statement false. Replacing the absolute word *all* with the qualified word *some* in the second statement makes the statement true.

    All metals are solid at room temperature.

    Some metals are solid at room temperature.

- **If you are uncertain whether a statement is true or false, make your best guess unless there is a penalty for incorrect answers.** If there is a penalty for incorrect answers, then answer only the questions for which you are certain about the answer. Guessing may not be beneficial to you. If there is no penalty for incorrect answers and you cannot make even an educated guess, select *true.* Research has shown that *true* is more often the correct answer than is *false.*

Unit 8: Taking Tests

Activity 8-4: Doing Well on True/False Tests (continued)

Take the following true/false test. This test is based on the guidelines for taking true/false tests that are presented in this activity.

Directions: Circle TRUE or FALSE in front of each statement. There is a one-point deduction for each incorrect answer.

True	False	1.	Qualified statements are usually true.
True	False	2.	If there is a penalty for incorrect answers, make your best guess.
True	False	3.	Absolute statements are usually false.
True	False	4.	If a statement has two negatives, you should cross out one of the negatives.
True	False	5.	If you are not certain that a statement is false, do not consider it true.
True	False	6.	You should never reread a statement when taking a true/false test.
True	False	7.	Most parts of a statement must be true for the statement to be true.
True	False	8.	A negative word can completely change the meaning of a statement.
True	False	9.	It is easier to prove that a statement is true than to prove that it is false.
True	False	10.	All things being equal, more statements are true than false.

Score your test as your teacher goes over the answers with you. Subtract your number incorrect from your number correct to get your score for the test. Enter your score in the box below to see how well you did.

My Score _____

9-10 = Excellent

7-8 = Good

0-6 = Review the guidelines presented in this activity.

Activity 8-5: Demonstrating Mastery of True/False Tests

Read the following information about India.

> India is located in South Asia, where it fronts the Bay of Bengal on the southeast and the Arabian Sea on the southwest. It is a consitutional republic consisting of 28 states, 6 union territories, and the Delhi national capital territory, which includes New Delhi, its capital. India is the second most populous country, after China. Direct administration by England began in 1858. After Mohandas Ghandi helped end British rule in 1947, Jawaharlal Nehru became India's first prime minister. India is one of the most ethnically diverse countries in the world. It is home to many religions and sects, innumerable castes and tribes, and hundreds of major and minor linguistic groups from several language families that are unrelated to one another. India has played an increasing role in global affairs in recent years. It has a well-developed infrastructure and a highly diversified industrial base. Its pool of scientists and engineers is one of the largest in the world. India's cultural impact is seen in its exports of music, literature, and cinema. India has expanded its agricultural base, and even today, the country's population remains largely rural.

Based on the information you just read about India, write true/false items as directed.

1. Write an item that is a qualified statement.

   _____

2. Write an item that contains a negative word or term.

   _____

3. Write an item in which everything in the statement is true.

   _____

4. Write an item that is an absolute statement.

   _____

5. Write an item in which at least one part of the statement is not true.

   _____

6. Write an item that contains two negatives.

   _____

Unit 8: Taking Tests

Activity 8-6: Learning About Matching Tests

Activity 8-6: Learning About Matching Tests

A **matching** test requires you to match items in a left-hand column (first column) with items in a right-hand column (second column). The items in the first column are termed *premises* and are assigned numbers. The items in the second column are called *responses* and are assigned letters (typically capital letters).

Here is an example of a matching test for which the answers are provided.

Directions: On the line next to each person in the first column, write the letter of the accomplishment of that person. Use each accomplishment just once.

    Person   **Accomplishment**

1. __D__ Thomas Edison   A. Composed famous waltzes

2. __A__ Johann Strauss   B. Developed polio vaccine

3. __C__ George Washington   C. First president of the United States

4. __B__ Jonas Salk   D. Patented many inventions

Sometimes there are more items in the second column than in the first column. This means that not every item in the second column can be used as a match for an item in the first column. Here is an example of this type of matching test with the answers provided.

Directions: On the line to the left of each writer in the first column, write the letter of the genre in which that person is known for writing. Do not use a genre more than once.

    Writer   **Genre**

1. __D__ Agatha Christie   A. Children's books

2. __E__ Stephen King   B. Humor

3. __A__ Dr. Seuss   C. Religion

4. __B__ Erma Bombeck   D. Mystery

5. __G__ Ray Bradbury   E. Horror

                                   F. Romance

                                   G. Science fiction

Unit 8: Taking Tests

Activity 8-6: Learning About Matching Tests (continued)

Read the following information about world capitals.

> Quite often the capital city of a country is famous, such as Paris, France. Here are some capitals that are not very well known in their own right: Nicosia, Cypress; Accra, Ghana; Doha, Qatar; Zagreb, Croatia; Reykjavik, Iceland. There are many capitals that you have probably never heard of such as the following: Monrovia, Liberia; Ulaanbaatar, Mongolia; Dhaka, Bangladesh; Antananarivo, Madagascar. The challenge is not only to remember these capitals, but to spell them as well.

Use this information to write a matching test in which capitals are to be matched to countries. Include at least six items, with more capitals than countries. Do not forget to include directions for taking the test. Use the space below to write your test.

Unit 8: Taking Tests

Activity 8-7: Doing Well on Matching Tests

Activity 8-7: Doing Well on Matching Tests

Here are some guidelines that will help you to do your best when taking a matching test. Read these guidelines and use them when you take the practice matching test in this activity and whenever you take matching tests given by your teachers.

- **Read all of the words or terms in both columns before making any matches.** If you make the first match that looks correct, you may not choose the correct match.

- **Start by making matches for the information about which you are certain.** This will reduce the number of choices for the matches about which you are not certain.

- **Cross out items in both columns as you make matches.** This reduces the information you will have to consider when making subsequent matches.

- **Make your best guess at the remaining matches only when there is no penalty for incorrect matches.** If there is a penalty for incorrect answers, then make matches only when you are certain they are correct. Guessing may not be beneficial.

- **Carefully review your matches when you have completed the test.** Reviewing the matches you made is important because an incorrect match may result in another match being incorrect.

Unit 8: Taking Tests

Activity 8-7: Doing Well on Matching Tests (continued)

Take the following matching test about the guidelines for taking matching tests you learned about in this activity.

Directions: On the line to the left of each Beginning of a guideline for taking matching tests, write the letter found next to the Ending that completes the guideline. There is no penalty for incorrect matches.

Beginning

1. _____ Read all the words or terms in both columns

2. _____ Make your best guess for the remaining matches

3. _____ Cross out items in both columns

4. _____ Start by making matches

5. _____ Carefully review your matches

Ending

a. when you have completed the test.

b. before making any matches.

c. only after you have made your matches.

d. only when there is no penalty for incorrect answers.

e. that seem the most difficult.

f. for the information about which you are certain.

g. as you make matches.

Score your test as your teacher goes over the answers with you. Your score is your number correct. Enter your score in the box below to see how well you did.

My score _____

5 = Excellent

4 = Good

0-3 = Review the guidelines presented in this activity.

Unit 8: Taking Tests

Activity 8-8: Learning About Completion Tests

Activity 8-8: Learning About Completion Tests

A **completion** test consists of statements that have one or more parts missing. A missing part of a statement can be anywhere in the statement and is shown by a blank line. You are required to complete the statement by writing the correct word or words on the blank line.

Here are examples of completion test items in which missing parts appear in different parts of the statements. The corrct answers are shown in (   ).

1. Of the 4,000 to 5,000 languages in the world, (Chinese) is the language spoken by the greatest number of people.

2. (Cheetahs) can run faster than any other animal.

3. The main reproductive parts of a flower are the female (carpel) and the male (stamen).

Read the following information about the city of Philadelphia.

Philadelphia was founded by William Penn in 1682. It is located in southeastern Pennsylvania, at the confluence of the Delaware and Schuylkill rivers. Philadephia was the capital of Pennsylvania from 1683-1789 and the capital of the United States between 1790 and 1800. Philadelphia's population grew in the 18th century, with many immigrants from Scotland, Ireland, and Germany. Philadelphia was the largest and most important city in the United States during the 19th century and was a center of the antislavery movement prior to the Civil War. The Pennsylvania Hospital founded in Philadelphia in 1751 was the first hospital in the United States. Philadelphia is also the site of the oldest art museum in the nation; the Pennsylvania Academy of the Fine Arts was founded there in 1805. Philadelphia was the birth place of American banking, and the first building and loan association was founded there. One of the first subway systems in the United States was established in this city in 1907. Philadelphia is very proud of the privately endowed University of Pennsylvania which was founded there in 1740. This university opened the nation's first medical school in 1765. If you are in Philadelphia, be sure to visit the Philadelphia Zoo. This zoo was founded in 1740 and is the oldest zoo in the country. Be sure to check out its 1,600 specimens representing 400 species.

Unit 8: Taking Tests

Activity 8-8: Learning About Completion Tests (continued)

Write a six-item completion test based on the information you just read about Philadelphia. Place your blank lines in different parts of the statement. At least one of your items should have two or more blank lines. Write the test in the space provided here.

Unit 8: Taking Tests

Activity 8-9: Guidelines for Taking Completion Tests

Activity 8-9: Guidelines for Taking Completion Tests

Here are some guidelines that will help you to do your best when taking a completion test. Read these guidelines and use them when you take the practice completion test in this activity and whenever you take completion tests given by your teachers.

- **Read the statement and try to identify the information that is missing.** On a piece of scrap paper or in the margins of the test paper, write several pieces of information that you think may be missing from the statement.

- **Select the answer that best completes the statement.** Review the information you wrote on scrap paper or on the test paper. Select and write the information that you think best completes the statement.

- **Read the completed statement to be sure it makes sense.** If the completed statement does not make sense with the information you wrote, replace what you wrote with other information you wrote on scrap paper or the test paper.

- **Read the completed statement once more to be sure it is grammatically correct.** If the completed statement is not grammatically correct, what you wrote is probably incorrect and needs to be changed.

- **Use the length of the blank line as a clue to the length of the answer.** Short blank lines may mean that only one word is needed to complete the statement. Longer blank lines may mean that more than one word is needed to complete the statement. This guideline does not work when the length of each blank line is the same throughout the test.

- **Do not guess at an answer when there is a penalty for incorrect answers.** This guideline is particularly important for completion tests because you must produce the correct answer rather than just recognize it. Having to produce an answer increases the possibility that your guess will be incorrect.

Unit 8: Taking Tests

Activity 8-9: Guidelines for Taking Completion Tests (continued)

Take the following completion test. This test is based on the guidelines for taking completion tests that you learned about in this activity.

Directions: Complete each statement by writing the missing word or words on the blank line or lines. There is no penalty for incorrect answers.

1. The completed statement should be _____ correct.

2. Use the length of the _____ as a clue to the length of the answer.

3. Guessing at the answer to a completion test item may not be _____ to you when there is a _____ for incorrect answers.

4. Write the answer that best completes the _____.

5. Read the statement and _____ about what information could be missing.

6. Sometimes the answer is one word; sometimes it is _____.

7. _____ the entire statement including your written answer to be sure it makes sense.

Score your test as your teacher goes over the answers with you. Your score is your number correct. Enter your score in the box below to see how well you did.

My score _____

7 = Excellent

5-6 = Good

0-4 = Review the guidelines presented in this activity.

266

Unit 8: Taking Tests

Activity 8-10: Learning About Essay Tests

Activity 8-10: Learning About Essay Tests

An **essay test** requires you to respond to items by using extended writing. You must recall and organize information you know in order to respond to an essay test item.

Here are the steps to follow when responding to an essay test item.

Step 1. Read the essay test item to learn what you must do.

Sometimes an essay test item is presented as a question that you must answer. Here is an example of an essay test item that is presented as a question.

How does electricity make your life easier?

Often an essay test item is presented as a statement containing a direction word that tells you what you must do to respond to the item. Here is an example of this type of item. It contains the direction word *justify*.

Justify the need for inspection of food processing plants.

You will learn about this direction word and others in others in Activity 8-11. It is a good idea to underline the direction word so that you focus your attention on what it tells you to do.

Step 2. Think about the information you should include in your response. It is helpful to write some notes on a piece of scrap paper or on a corner or back of the test page.

Step 3. Organize the information into an outline that contains main ideas and supporting details. Number the main ideas in the order in which you plan to include them in your response. For each main idea, number the supporting details in the order in which you plan to present them.

Step 4. Write your response. Write legibly so that your teacher can easily read your response. Begin with an introduction in which you state your main point to be made and how you intend to respond to the item. Keep your introduction short. The bulk of your time should be spent on responding to what is asked by elaborating on the information you orgranized in Step 3. Use language that is clear and direct. Be sure to include all of the important information. Where appropriate include terms used in your textbook and by your teacher. Provide as many examples and facts as possible to support what you write. Conclude your response by restating both your main idea and what you did to respond to the item.

Unit 8: Taking Tests

Activity 8-10: Learning About Essay Tests (continued)

Step 5. Reread your response to make sure that you responded to what the item required.

Step 6. Check your spelling, grammar, and punctuation. Some teachers deduct points for errors in these writing mechanics.

Answer these questions.

1. Does every test item include a direction word?

2. If you are not allowed to use scrap paper, where can you write your notes?

3. Why should you check your spelling, grammar, and punctuation?

4. What should your introduction consist of?

5. How should you organize the information you will include in your response?

6. What should your conclusion consist of?

7. Why should you reread your response to an item?

8. Do essay test items require you to recognize information, or do they require you to recall information?

Activity 8-11: Direction Words in Essay Test Items

As noted in Activity 8-10, essay test items are often presented as a statement that contains a **direction word**. Here are common direction words you will often find in essay test items. Read the list below to learn what each direction word tells you to do. An example of an essay test item that contains the direction word is provided.

Analyze Break something into its separate parts. Show how the parts relate to each other to make the whole.

Analyze how blood circulates through the human body.

Compare Tell how two or more things are similar and different.

Compare electrical energy and nuclear energy.

Contrast Tell how two or more things are different.

Contrast the platform of the Republican Party with that of the Democratic Party.

Discuss Consider and debate or argue the pros and cons of an issue.

Discuss the proposal of some scientists that the United States should expand its space exploration efforts.

Define Explain the meaning of something in a brief manner.

Define what is meant by the expression "two heads are better than one."

Describe Present a full and detailed picture of something in words. Include information about the characteristics of the thing you are describing.

Describe what it must have been like to live during the Great Depression.

Explain Provide reasons and facts to make something very clear and understandable.

Explain the system of checks and balances in American goverment.

Illustrate Provide concrete examples to explain something.

Illustrate the ways in which world governments are dealing with the problem of global warming.

Justify   Tell why something is correct.

Justify the need for stricter penalties for violent crimes.

List   Present information as a series of brief numbered points.

List the steps you should follow to prepare for college.

Summarize   Present the main points about something in a brief form.

Summarize what you need to do in order to succeed in high school.

Support   Provide an argument to back something up. Use facts and logic in your argument.

Support the need to maintain the electoral college system.

Trace   Tell the order of events for something.

Trace the events that led to the American Civil War.

For each of the following, write the direction word that is most appropriate. You can use a direction word more than once.

1. Your teacher wants you to briefly tell what photosynthesis means.

   _____

2. Your teacher wants you to identify five characteristics of mammals.

   _____

3. Your teacher wants you to present a case for Shakespeare being the greatest writer of all time.

   _____

4. Your teacher wants you to break down into parts or steps the process by which wood pulp is made into paper.

   _____

5. Your teacher wants you to tell what a tropical rain forest is like.

   _____

Unit 8: Taking Tests

Activity 8-11: Direction Words in Essay Test Items (continued)

6. Your teacher wants you to tell how a democracy and a monarchy are different.

   _____

7. Your teacher wants you to present clear facts about the duties of the president of the United States.

   _____

8. Your teacher wants you to tell how lions and tigers are alike and different.

   _____

9. Your teacher wants you to tell the sequence of steps to follow when answering an essay test item.

   _____

10. Your teacher wants you to briefly tell the most important points about how a person is elected to be the president of the United States.

    _____

11. Your teacher wants you to state very clearly what the SAT assesses.

    _____

12. Your teacher wants you to tell the order of the events that led up to the resignation of President Richard Nixon.

    _____

13. Your teacher wants you to present a very full and detailed description of how a hot air balloon works.

    _____

14. Your teacher wants you to write about your position regarding capital punishment.

    _____

15. Your teacher wants you to provide examples of how the World Health Organization has benefitted people around the world.

    _____

Unit 8: Taking Tests

Activity 8-12: Practice Writing a Response to an Essay Test Item

Activity 8-12: Practice Writing a Response to an Essay Test Item

In Activity 8-10 you learned about six steps to follow when responding to an essay test item. Use what you learned to write a response to the following item.

Analyze what you should do when responding to an essay test item.

Unit 8: Taking Tests

Activity 8-13: Reviewing Your Response to an Essay Test Item

Activity 8-13: Reviewing Your Response to an Essay Test Item

Review your response to the essay test item you wrote in Activity 8-12. Circle **Yes** or **No** for each of the following questions about your response.

Did I respond to the question or do what the direction word required me to do?	**Yes**	**No**
If the item included a direction word, did I underline the direction word?	**Yes**	**No**
Did I prepare an outline containing main ideas and supporting details?	**Yes**	**No**
Did I include all important information?	**Yes**	**No**
Did I begin with an introduction?	**Yes**	**No**
Did I write notes on scrap paper or on the test paper?	**Yes**	**No**
Did I end with a conclusion?	**Yes**	**No**
Did I write legibly?	**Yes**	**No**
Did I reread my response to make sure I responded to what the item required?	**Yes**	**No**
Did I check for correct grammar?	**Yes**	**No**
Did I check for correct punctuation?	**Yes**	**No**
Did I check for correct spelling?	**Yes**	**No**

Any question for which your answer is **No** is something you should be very careful about when you take essay tests.

> Unit 8: Taking Tests
>
> Activity 8-14: What I Have Learned

Activity 8-14: What I Have Learned

Read the following information about the Earth's climate.

The Earth's Climate

Many people think that weather and climate are the same thing. This is not true. Weather is the atmospheric conditions for a place at a given time. Climate is the general weather conditions for a place or region over a long period of time (a period of at least thirty years). If you think about it, over time you have acquired an impression of the climate in the place where you live. If you look at national weather reports over time, you will acquire an impression of climate in many places in the United States. For example, in Minneapolis, Minnesota, the climate is most often cold in the winter and mild in the summer. In Miami, Florida, the climate is most often mild in the winter and hot in the summer.

Factors That Determine Climate

Temperature and precipitation are the two major determiners of climatic conditions anywhere on Earth.

Temperature. One of the major determiners of climate is temperature. Temperature is measured using a thermometer in degrees Fahrenheit in the United States and degrees Celsius in many other places in the world. The higher the temperature is in a place over time, the hotter the climatic conditions will be. Likewise, the lower the temperature is in a place over time, the colder the climatic conditions will be. Temperature makes the difference between hot and cold climatic conditions.

Precipitation. The second major determiner of weather is precipitation. Precipitation occurs in a variety of forms: rain, snow, hail, and sleet. Precipitation is measured in inches in the United States and in centimeters in many other places in the world. Little or no precipitation results in deserts where very little vegetation grows. A moderate amount of precipitation helps to produce an abundance of vegetation and crops. Too much precipitation can produce flooding in which overflowing rivers wash away seeds and the soil that holds the seeds. Precipitation makes the difference between dry and wet climatic conditions.

Major Factors That Influence Climate

You have already learned that temperature and precipitation determine climate. Four major factors that influence temperature and precipitation, and therefore influence climate, are: latitude, altitude, topography, and ocean currents. These factors create a variety of environments such as deserts, tropical rain forests, tundra, conifer forests, prairies, plains, glacial ice, and others.

Latitude. The equator is an imaginary line that divides the earth into north and south. Latitude is how distance is measured going north and south from the equator. The equator is at zero degrees latitude. Ninety degrees latitude north of the equator is the North Pole, and ninety degrees latitude south of the equator is the South Pole. Areas close to the equator receive direct rays from the sun. This results in a warm climate. In areas that are close to the poles, the rays of the sun are at an angle. This results in a cold climate. The closer one gets to the equator, the warmer the climate. The farther one gets from the equator, the colder the climate.

Altitude. Altitude is the distance above sea level. As altitude increases, air pressure decreases and the air becomes less dense. The less dense the air, the less heat it holds. Therefore, the higher the altitude, the lower the temperature. Air temperature drops approximately 3.5 degrees Fahrenheit per 1,000 feet of altitude. Altitude affects precipitation as well as air temperature. The higher the altitude, the more likely rain will become snow or ice.

Topography. When you are reading, talking, or writing about the surface features of the earth, you are studying topography. Topography can be flat lands, rolling hills, mountains, or any feature on the surface of the earth. These surface features affect the development of clouds and precipitation. For example, as humid air moves up a mountainside, clouds are formed from the water in the air. These water-laden clouds can eventually produce rain, snow, or ice.

Ocean Currents. Water in the oceans of the world travels in paths. These paths are called currents, and they can be warm or cold. Warm water heats the air above it. Cold water cools the air above it. Ocean currents moving away from the equator are warm. They bring with them heated air masses that raise the temperatures over the regions in their path. Currents moving toward the equator are colder. They bring with them cooled air masses that lower the temperatures over the regions in their path.

Types of Climates

Wladimir Köppen was a Russian/German climatologist who in 1900 introduced a system for classifying the climates of the world. His system remains in wide use today. Köppen recognized five major climate types based on annual and monthly averages of temperature and precipitation. Climate types in Köppen's system are identified by the upper case letters **A**, **B**, **C**, **D**, and **E**.

Unit 8: Taking Tests

Activity 8-14: What I Have Learned (continued)

A—Moist Tropical Climate. This climate has high temperatures throughout the year. It receives a large amount of rainfall year round.

B—Dry Climate. This climate receives little rain. The range of daily temperatures is very large.

C—Humid Middle Latitude Climate. This climate is warm and dry in the summer. In the winter, it is cool and wet.

D—Continental Climate. This climate is typically found in the interior regions of large masses of land. Total precipitation is not very high. Temperatures vary widely across the seasons.

E—Cold Climate. This climate occurs in areas where ice is always present. Freezing temperatures occur for most of the year.

Summary

Climate is the general weather conditions for a place or region over a long period. Temperature and precipitation are the two major determinants of climate. Four major factors that influence temperature and precipitation are latitude, altitude, topography, and ocean currents. Wladimir Köppen introduced a system for classifying climates in 1900. His system, which is still widely used, recognized the following five major climate types: moist tropical, dry, humid middle latitude, continental, and cold.

Based on the passage about the earth's climate, write each of the following test items.

1. A multiple-choice item in the form of an incomplete statement followed by four answer choices:

    Statement: _____

    a. _____

    b. _____

    c. _____

    d. _____

Unit 8: Taking Tests

Activity 8-14: What I Have Learned (continued)

2. A multiple-choice item in the form of a question followed by five answer choices.

   Question: _____

   a. _____

   b. _____

   c. _____

   d. _____

3. A true/false item.

   _____

4. A matching test with four items in the left-hand column and five in the right-hand column.

   Directions: _____

   Heading _____   Heading _____

   1. _____   a. _____

   2. _____   b. _____

   3. _____   c. _____

   4. _____   d. _____

                                         e. _____

5. A completion test item with the missing part at the end.

   _____

6. A completion test item with two missing parts.

   _____

7. An essay test item that contains a question to be answered.

   _____

8. An essay test item that contains the direction word *explain*.

   _____

Unit 9
Building Vocabulary Through Word Meaning Clues

Activities

9-1   Definition Clues to Word Meaning

9-2   Synonym Clues to Word Meaning

9-3   Antonym Clues to Word Meaning

9-4   Adage Clues to Word Meaning

9-5   Identifying Clues to Word Meaning

9-6   Visual Clues to Word Meaning

9-7   Learning About the Vocabulary Building Strategy

9-8   Using My Vocabulary Words

9-9   Practice Using the Vocabulary Building Strategy: Social Studies

9-10 Practice Using the Vocabulary Building Strategy: Science

9-11 What I Have Learned

Unit 9: Building Vocabulary Through Word Meaning Clues

Activity 9-1: Definition Clues to Word Meaning

Activity 9-1: Definition Clues to Word Meaning

While reading your textbooks, you will at times come to a word whose meaning you are unsure about or you do not know. Textbook writers frequently provide clues to the meanings of words they think their readers may need help understanding. Recognizing and using word meaning clues provided by writers will help you to build your vocabulary as well as to increase your comprehension of what you are reading.

In this unit you will learn about the following five types of **word meaning clues** that writers use: definition clues, synonym clues, antonym clues, adage clues, and visual clues. In this activity you will learn about **definition clues**.

> A **definition clue** is two or more words that tell the meaning of a word whose meaning the reader might need to learn.

Sometimes a writer presents a word and its definition clue within the same sentence. Read the sentence that follows.

Sam heard the *reverberating* sound of his voice *repeatedly reflected* off the mountain.

Notice how the writer provided the definition clue *repeatedly reflected* to help the reader understand the meaning of *reverberating*. Once you identify a definition clue, the meaning of the word it refers to will be apparent.

Other times a writer provides a definition clue for an unknown word in the next sentence. Read the following two sentences.

The *blaring* sound came from a nearby car radio. The *extremely loud sound* could be heard all over the neighborhood.

Notice how the writer provided the definition clue *extremely loud sound* in the second sentence to help the reader understand the meaning of the word *blaring* that appeared in the first sentence.

Unit 9: Building Vocabulary Through Word Meaning Clues

Activity 9-1: Definition Clues to Word Meaning (continued)

A word is underlined in each of the following items. Read each item to find the definition clue provided by the writer to help the reader learn the meaning of the underlined word. Then write the definition clue.

1. Throughout your life, you will often meet with <u>adversity</u>. In the course of living, you can expect an unfortunate circumstance to occur from time to time.

   Definition Clue: _____

2. A student council president should <u>embody</u> the qualities of leadership, organization, spirit, and free expression. Student government candidates must clearly exhibit these qualities.

   Definition Clue: _____

3. In order to <u>accelerate</u> help for the hurricane victims, the relief workers were encouraged to increase the speed of their activities.

   Definition Clue: _____

4. Allan is incapable of <u>discerning</u> right from wrong. Frank, on the other hand, is able to recognize the difference between appropriate and inappropriate behavior.

   Definition Clue: _____

5. Susan's <u>fortuitous</u> meeting with the movie director was yet another example of how her acting success has been characterized by fortunate events of chance.

   Definition Clue: _____

6. Roger found the exercise to be <u>odious</u>, arousing his strong dislike for strenuous physical activity.

   Definition Clue: _____

7. Elizabeth was fond of <u>epigrams</u>. She loved to read these short, witty poems.

   Definition Clue: _____

8. The police responded with <u>exigency</u>. They knew that the situation required immediate action.

   Definition Clue: _____

Unit 9: Building Vocabulary Through Word Meaning Clues

Activity 9-2: Synonym Clues to Word Meaning

Activity 9-2: Synonym Clues to Word Meaning

Synonym clues are a second way that writers help readers learn the meanings of words. A synonym is a word that has the same meaning or nearly the same meaning as another word. For example, *stop* is a synonym for *prevent*.

> A **synonym clue** is a word that has the same or nearly the same meaning as a word whose meaning the reader might need to learn.

Sometimes a writer presents a word and its synonym clue within the same sentence. Read the sentence that follows.

What she said was so *implausible* that it was *unbelievable*.

Notice how the writer provided the synonym clue *unbelievable* to help the reader understand the meaning of *implausible*. Once you identify a synonym clue, the meaning of the word it refers to will be apparent.

Other times a writer provides a synonym clue for an unknown word in the next sentence. Read the following two sentences.

There was considerable *strife* between the two contestants. Their *rivalry* was easy to see in their facial expressions as they competed for the trophy.

Notice how the writer provided the synonym clue *rivalry* in the second sentence to help the reader understand the meaning of the word *strife* that appeared in the first sentence.

A word is underlined in each of the following items. Read each item to find the synonym clue the writer provided to help the reader learn the meaning of the underlined word. Then write the synonym clue.

1. Paul's behavior was an <u>enigma</u>. It seemed that it was a mystery that would never be solved.

   Synonym Clue: _____

2. His <u>fallacious</u> argument was quickly shown to be false.

   Synonym Clue: _____

Unit 9: Building Vocabulary Through Word Meaning Clues

Activity 9-2: Synonym Clues to Word Meaning (continued)

3. As soon as the comedian began his performance, a man from the audience started to heckle him. The man continued to annoy the comedian until he was removed by the security guards.

   Synonym Clue: _____

4. The captain demanded the fidelity of his crew. Loyalty was something he valued.

   Synonym Clue: _____

5. My intuition tells me this will be a lucky day for me. Whenever I have this insight, something good happens.

   Synonym Clue: _____

6. There was mirth among all who came to the graduation party. The celebration was filled with merriment.

   Synonym Clue: _____

7. The scientist expected more than conjecture or a guess when Frank responded to his question.

   Synonym Clue: _____

8. Susan was thrilled that the illustrious writer would be visiting her English class. She thought it would be great to meet a famous person.

   Synonym Clue: _____

9. Helene approached the test day with nonchalance. Her indifference was surprising to her friends.

   Synonym Clue: _____

10. The mountain climber had a precarious grip on the edge of the cliff. His insecure grip posed a great danger.

    Synonym Clue: _____

11. The ordinance was not a well received regulation.

    Synonym Clue: _____

12. Carl responded to the crisis in an impetuous manner. He was later sorry for being so hasty.

    Synonym Clue: _____

Activity 9-3: Antonym Clues to Word Meaning

Antonym clues are a third way that writers help readers learn the meanings of words. An antonym is a word that has the opposite or nearly the opposite meaning of another word. For example, *busy* is an antonym for *idle*.

> An **antonym clue** is a word that has the opposite or nearly the opposite meaning of a word whose meaning the reader might need to learn.

Sometimes a writer presents a word and its antonym clue within the same sentence. Read the sentence that follows.

> An *arid* climate does not support good crop growth, but *humid* conditions are excellent for growing tropical fruits and vegetables.

Notice how the writer provided the antonym clue *humid* to show that *arid* means the opposite of *humid*. That is, *arid* means dry.

Other times a writer provides an antonym clue for an unknown word in the next sentence. Read the following two sentences.

> Jose often felt *dejected* on rainy days. He preferred sunny days since he usually felt *happy* when the sky was bright.

Notice how the writer provided the antonym clue *happy* in the second sentence to show that *dejected* means the opposite of *happy*. That is, *dejected* means sad.

A word is underlined in each of the following items. Read each item to find the antonym clue provided by the writer to help the reader learn the meaning of the underlined word. Then write the antonym clue followed by what you think the underlined word means.

1. The coach <u>chastised</u> the players for allowing the opposing team to score, but he praised them for showing good sportsmanship.

    Antonym Clue: _____

    Meaning of chastised: _____

284

Unit 9: Building Vocabulary Through Word Meaning Clues

Activity 9-3: Antonym Clues to Word Meaning (continued)

2. The director of the organization wants to employ <u>diligent</u> students from high school service organizations to collect canned goods for the needy during the Thanksgiving break. He will dismiss any student he finds to be lazy.

   Antonym Clue: _____

   Meaning of diligent: _____

3. The people were tired of a government that was a <u>tyranny</u>. They wanted a government that was a democracy.

   Antonym Clue: _____

   Meaning of tyranny: _____

4. My friend made <u>disparaging</u> remarks as the visiting team entered the gymnasium. I was surprised because he is usually very complimentary in what he says about others.

   Antonym Clue: _____

   Meaning of disparaging: _____

5. The <u>dissidence</u> between the two partners was alarming because they almost always were in agreement on important matters.

   Antonym Clue: _____

   Meaning of dissidence: _____

6. The teacher was alarmed by the <u>boisterous</u> behavior of the class. She much preferred to teach a class that was quiet.

   Antonym Clue: _____

   Meaning of boisterous: _____

7. The soup mix will <u>congeal</u> if you put it in the refrigerator but will liquefy if you leave it out on the counter.

   Antonym Clue: _____

   Meaning of congeal: _____

Activity 9-4: Adage Clues To Word Meaning

Adage clues are a fourth way that writers help readers learn the meanings of words. An adage is a saying that has gained popularity through long use. It does not have literal meaning. For example, *pie in the sky* is an adage that has come to mean that something is *farfetched* or *outrageous*.

> An **adage clue** is a familiar saying that helps the reader learn the meaning of a word whose meaning the reader might not know.

Sometimes a writer presents a word and its adage clue within the same sentence. Read the sentence that follows.

> Harriet was a *nonconformist* who people said *marched to a different drummer*.

Notice how the writer provided the adage clue *marched to a different drummer* to help the reader understand the meaning of *nonconformist*. The adage clue *marched to a different drummer* brought out that *nonconformist* means someone who does things in his or her own way and does not follow what everyone else does.

Other times a writer provides an adage clue for an unknown word in the next sentence. Read the following two sentences.

> Because they both liked to collect stamps, George and Susan had an *affinity* for each other. As in all things, *birds of a feather flock together*.

Notice how the writer provided the adage clue *birds of a feather flock together* in the second sentence to help the reader understand the word *affinity* that appeared in the first sentence. The adage clue *birds of a feather flock together* brought out that *affinity* means a natural attraction or feeling of kinship based on some similarity.

Unit 9: Building Vocabulary Through Word Meaning Clues

Activity 9-4: Adage Clues To Word Meaning (continued)

A word is underlined in each of the following items. Read each item to find the adage clue provided by the writer to help the reader learn the meaning of the underlined word. Then write the adage clue followed by what you think the underlined word means.

1. Rosanna knew that the rumor she heard was <u>unassailable</u>. Hearing it from the chairman of the committee was getting it straight from the horse's mouth.

   Adage Clue: _____

   Meaning of unassailable: _____

2. As an engineer, I have always been very <u>methodical</u> about my work because haste makes waste.

   Adage Clue: _____

   Meaning of methodical: _____

3. Henry was a <u>sanguine</u> person. Even in the worst of times, he believed that all things must pass.

   Adage Clue: _____

   Meaning of sanguine: _____

4. Tom felt very <u>queasy</u> as he stood up. He was definitely under the weather.

   Adage Clue: _____

   Meaning of queasy: _____

5. William was not about to let himself be <u>bamboozled</u> once again. No one was going to pull the wool over his eyes this time.

   Adage Clue: _____

   Meaning of bamboozled: _____

6. Jim's <u>contentious</u> attitude caused people to say that he always had a chip on his shoulder.

   Adage Clue: _____

   Meaning of contentious: _____

Activity 9-5: Identifying Clues to Word Meaning

You have learned how writers use Definition Clues, Synonym Clues, Antonym Clues, and Adage Clues to help readers learn the meanings of words. Now see how well you are able to identify these clues.

Read each of the following items. For each item, circle the type of clue used by the writer to help the reader learn the meaning of the underlined word.

1. The letter from my mother was <u>ambiguous</u> as to the time and nature of the appointment, so I called her to be clear about the details.

    Definition   Synonym   Antonym   Adage

2. A person with your experience is <u>valuable</u> to us. Anyone without experience is worthless to the team.

    Definition   Synonym   Antonym   Adage

3. The meal was <u>delectable</u>. Seldom do you get an opportunity to taste such delicious food.

    Definition   Synonym   Antonym   Adage

4. The summer <u>solstice</u> is on June 21 in the northern hemisphere. This is the date on which the sun is farthest north of the equator.

    Definition   Synonym   Antonym   Adage

5. The <u>attrition</u> rate in the marathon was very high. The runners were dropping like flies.

    Definition   Synonym   Antonym   Adage

6. Stop that <u>hullabaloo</u> right now! That noise is giving me a headache.

    Definition   Synonym   Antonym   Adage

7. The English teacher told the class members to be <u>concise</u> in their writing. She wanted them to cut to the chase.

    Definition   Synonym   Antonym   Adage

8. Laura found the homework assignment <u>perplexing</u>. She thought that the directions were puzzling and confusing.

    Definition   Synonym   Antonym   Adage

Unit 9: Building Vocabulary Through Word Meaning Clues

Activity 9-6: Visual Clues to Word Meaning

Activity 9-6: Visual Clues to Word Meaning

Visual clues are a fifth way that writers help readers learn the meanings of words. Visual clues are different from the other meaning clues you learned about because pictures, drawings, and illustrations are used to provide clues to meaning.

> A **visual clue** is a picture, drawing, or illustration to help the reader learn the meaning of a word whose meaning the reader might not know.

A visual clue is placed as close as possible to the word it refers to. Read the following sentence and then examine the picture to see how the writer used a visual clue to help the reader learn the meaning of *frown* as a facial expression of displeasure.

The <u>frown</u> on his face revealed his true feelings.

Keep in mind that not all pictures, drawings, or illustrations are visual clues. Some simply are there to provide interest or to add to the visual appeal of what is written.

A word is underlined in each of the items that start on the next page. Read each item and then examine the visual clue to help you learn the meaning of the word. Then write what you think the underlined word means.

Unit 9: Building Vocabulary Through Word Meaning Clues

Activity 9-6: Visual Clues to Word Meaning (continued)

1. As he steered his boat, Tom's father watched for a <u>buoy</u> that would warn him of a hazard in the water.

   Meaning of buoy: _____

   _____

2. Helen's mother liked the furnishings of the dining room except for the <u>chandelier</u>.

   Meaning of chandelier: _____

   _____

3. He was interested in all kinds of things that were of Russian origin, especially the <u>balalaika</u>.

   Meaning of balalaika: _____

   _____

Unit 9: Building Vocabulary Through Word Meaning Clues

Activity 9-6: Visual Clues to Word Meaning (continued)

4. Skin specialists recommend that you wear something like a <u>sombrero</u> when outside on a very sunny day.

   Meaning of sombrero: _____

5. Philip bought a <u>toboggan</u> to use during his winter vacation.

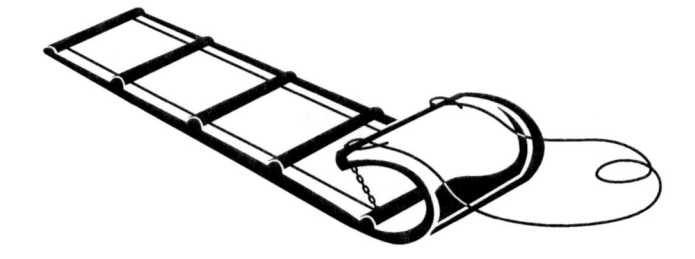

   Meaning of toboggan: _____

6. Sandra used a <u>gaff</u> to haul the big fish she caught into the boat.

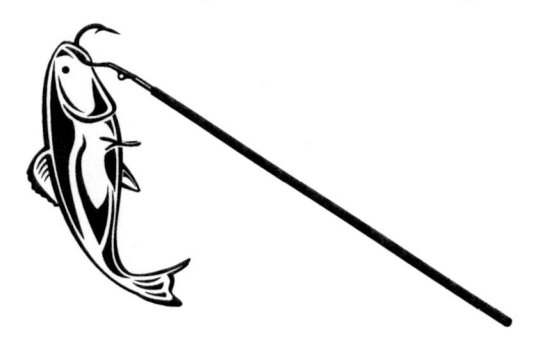

   Meaning of gaff: _____

Unit 9: Building Vocabulary Through Word Meaning Clues

Activity 9-6: Visual Clues to Word Meaning (continued)

7. He looked distinguished because of the monocle he wore.

   Meaning of monocle: _____

   _____

8. The orchestra conductor strode briskly to the podium.

   Meaning of podium: _____

   _____

Activity 9-7: Learning About the Vocabulary Building Strategy

In the previous activities in this unit, you learned about five types of clues to word meaning used by writers. In this activity you will learn to use a **vocabulary building strategy** that utilizes these clues to learn the meanings of words you are unsure about or do not know.

Here are the six steps in the vocabulary building strategy:

Step 1. Look for a clue to the meaning of the word. First, look to see if there is a visual clue. If there is no visual clue, examine the sentence in which the word appears and the sentence that follows to see if the writer provided one of the following clues: definition clue, synonym clue, antonym clue, adage clue. If a clue is provided, use the clue to learn the meaning of the word and skip to Step 3. If a clue is not provided, continue with Step 2.

Step 2. Look up the meaning of the word in the glossary of the textbook in which the word was used. The meaning of the word provided in the glossary is the meaning intended by the writer. If the textbook does not have a glossary, or the glossary does not include the word, look up the meaning of the word in a print or online dictionary. If you have to use a dictionary, be sure to select the meaning of the word that best fits the context of the sentence in which you came across the word while reading.

Step 3. Write the word and its meaning on a My Vocabulary Words form. You will learn how to use this form in Activity 9-8.

Step 4. Write the sentence from your textbook that included the word on the My Vocabulary Words form.

Step 5. Write your own sentence that includes the word on the My Vocabulary Words form. Writing a sentence using the word is a good way to be sure you really know the meaning of the word.

Step 6. Review the meaning of the word as often as possible. Record the date each time you review the word on the My Vocabulary Words form.

Use the following review procedure:

- Say the word.
- Say the meaning of the word.
- Use the word in a spoken sentence and in a written sentence.
- Explain the meaning of the word to someone else.

Unit 9: Building Vocabulary Through Word Meaning Clues

Activity 9-7: Learning About the Vocabulary Building Strategy (continued)

Answer these questions about using the vocabulary building strategy.

1. What five types of clues should you look for to help you learn the meaning of a word whose meaning you are unsure about or do not know?

   _____

2. Which one of these clues should you look for first?

   _____

3. Where can you look up the meanings of words?

   _____

4. When using a dictionary to learn the meaning of a word, what should you do if more than one meaning is provided for the word?

   _____

5. Once you learn the meaning of a word, where should you write the word and its meaning?

   _____

6. Why should you write your own sentence that includes the word?

   _____

7. How often should you review words you write on the My Vocabulary Words form?

   _____

8. Write what you should do in each step of the word meaning strategy.

   Step 1. _____

   _____

   _____

   _____

Unit 9: Building Vocabulary Through Word Meaning Clues

Activity 9-7: Learning About the Vocabulary Building Strategy (continued)

Step 2. _____
_____
_____
_____

Step 3. _____
_____
_____
_____

Step 4. _____
_____
_____
_____

Step 5. _____
_____
_____
_____

Step 6. _____
_____
_____
_____

Unit 9: Building Vocabulary Through Word Meaning Clues

Activity 9-8: Using My Vocabulary Words

Activity 9-8: Using My Vocabulary Words

Here are the steps to follow to use the **My Vocabulary Words form**.

1. Next to **Word**, write the word whose meaning you have just learned.

2. Next to **Meaning**, write the meaning of the word.

3. Next to **Sentence from Textbook**, write the sentence from your textbook that included the word.

4. Next to **Sentence**, write the word in a sentence.

5. Next to **Review Dates**, record the date each time you review the meaning of the word.

Here is an example of the use of the My Vocabulary Words form for the word *enlightened* as found in a high school history textbook.

My Vocabulary Words

Word: enlightened

Meaning: educated, informed

Sentence from Textbook: Liberals saw themselves as enlightened supporters of progress but often showed little concern for the needs of the majority of the people.

Your Own Sentence: My high school experience has enlightened me about the social issues facing the world today.

Review Dates: 2/7, 2/22, 3/8

Unit 9: Building Vocabulary Through Word Meaning Clues

Activity 9-8: Using My Vocabulary Words (continued)

Here are some sentences found in high school textbooks. Each sentence contains a word that is underlined. The meaning of the word is shown in parentheses following the sentence.

The most controversial new idea came from the British naturalist Charles Darwin. (something that is likely to be argued about or debated)

In the new atmosphere of emancipation, women pursued careers in many areas—from sports to the arts. (freedom from restrictions)

They reorganized the bureaucracy and system of tax collection. (govenment staffed by administrators and officials who follow rigid rules)

Historians still debate the real nature of Mussolini's fascist ideology. (a system of ideas that guides an individual, movement, or political program)

Governments had to subsidize part of the cost of importing food from overseas. (support with government spending)

Complete the rest of the My Vocabulary Words form below for each of the underlined words from the sentences above. You do not have to record review dates for this activity.

Word: _____

Meaning: _____

Sentence from Textbook: _____

Your Own Sentence: _____

Word: _____

Meaning: _____

Sentence from Textbook: _____

Your Own Sentence: _____

Unit 9: Building Vocabulary Through Word Meaning Clues

Activity 9-8: Using My Vocabulary Words (continued)

Word: _____

Meaning: _____

Sentence from Textbook: _____
_____

Your Own Sentence: _____
_____

Word: _____

Meaning: _____

Sentence from Textbook: _____
_____

Your Own Sentence: _____
_____

Word: _____

Meaning: _____

Sentence from Textbook: _____
_____

Your Own Sentence: _____
_____

A blank My Vocabulary form is provided on the following page. You can make copies of this form to use as needed.

Unit 9: Building Vocabulary Through Word Meaning Clues
Activity 9-8: Using My Vocabulary Words (continued)

My Vocabulary Words

Word: _____

Meaning: _____

Sentence from Textbook: _____
_____

Your Own Sentence: _____
_____

Review Dates: _____

Word: _____

Meaning: _____

Sentence from Textbook: _____
_____

Your Own Sentence: _____
_____

Review Dates: _____

Word: _____

Meaning: _____

Sentence from Textbook: _____
_____

Your Own Sentence: _____
_____

Review Dates: _____

Copyright Mangrum-Strichart Learning Resources
www.mangrum-strichart.com

Unit 9: Building Vocabulary Through Word Meaning Clues

Activity 9-9: Practice Using the Vocabulary Building Strategy: Social Studies

Activity 9-9: Practice Using the Vocabulary Building Strategy: Social Studies

Look in a social studies textbook to find a word whose meaning you do not know or are unsure about and for which there is no visual clue. Write the word here: _____

Write both the sentence containing the unknown word and the sentence that follows it here.

_____

_____

_____

Use the word meaning strategy to learn the meaning of the word you wrote. Use the blank My Vocabulary Words form provided in Activity 9-8 as needed.

Step 1.   Examine the two sentences you wrote to see if the writer provided a definition clue, synonym clue, antonym clue, or an adage clue to help you understand the meaning of the word. If one of these clues is provided, use the clue to learn the meaning of the word and skip to Step 3. If a clue is not provided, go to Step 2.

Step 2.   Look for the definition of the word in the glossary of your textbook if there is one. If there is no glossary or the word is not defined in the glossary, look up the definition of the word in a print or online dictionary. Be sure to select the meaning of the word in the dictionary that best fits the context of the sentence in which the word was used in your textbook.

Step 3.   Write the word and its meaning on the My Vocabulary Words form in Activity 9-8.

Step 4.   Write the sentence from the textbook that contains the unknown word on the My Vocabulary Words form.

Step 5.   Write your own sentence using the unknown word on the My Vocabulary Words form. Be sure to use the meaning of the word intended by the writer.

Step 6.   Review the meaning of the word as often as possible. Use the review procedure you learned in Activity 9-7. Each time you review the meaning of the unknown word, record the date on the My Vocabulary Words form.

Unit 9: Building Vocabulary Through Word Meaning Clues

Activity 9-10: Practice Using the Vocabulary Building Strategy: Science

Activity 9-10: Practice Using the Vocabulary Building Strategy: Science

Look in a science textbook to find a word whose meaning you do not know or are unsure about and for which there is no visual clue. Write the word here:

_____

Write both the sentence containing the word and the sentence that follows it here.

_____

_____

_____

Use the word meaning strategy to learn the meaning of the word you wrote. Use the blank My Vocabulary Words form provided in Activity 9-8 as needed.

Step 1.   Examine the two sentences you wrote to see if the writer provided a definition clue, synonym clue, antonym clue, or an adage clue to help you understand the meaning of the word. If one of these clues is provided, use the clue to learn the meaning of the word and skip to Step 3. If a clue is not provided, go to Step 2.

Step 2.   Look for the definition of the word in the glossary of your textbook if there is one. If there is no glossary or the word is not defined in the glossary, look up the definition of the word in a print or online dictionary. Be sure to select the meaning of the word in the dictionary that best fits the context of the sentence in which the word was used in your textbook.

Step 3.   Write the word and its meaning on the My Vocabulary Words form in Activity 9-8.

Step 4.   Write the sentence from the textbook that contains the unknown word on the My Vocabulary Words form.

Step 5.   Write your own sentence using the unknown word on the My Vocabulary Words form. Be sure to use the meaning of the word intended by the writer.

Step 6.   Review the meaning of the word as often as possible. Use the review procedure you learned in Activity 9-7. Each time you review the meaning of the word, record the date on the My Vocabulary Words form.

Activity 9-11: What I Have Learned

Answer the following questions about word meaning clues.

1. What is an adage clue?

   _____

2. What is a visual clue?

   _____

3. What is an antonym clue?

   _____

4. What is a definition clue?

   _____

5. What is a synonym clue?

   _____

Identify and write the type of word meaning clue provided for the underlined word in each of the following items.

6. The senator decided to use a <u>filibuster</u> to block the vote on the proposal he opposed. The other senators resented having to listen to his incredibly long speech.

   _____

7. Although he acknowledged that he was a <u>refugee</u>, Antonio resented being referred to as an alien.

   _____

8. Carolyn was known as a great <u>innovator</u>. Whenever others got stuck on a problem, Carolyn's willingness to go against the grain allowed her to come up with new ideas.

   _____

9. Matthew was a classic <u>omnivore</u> who ate both meat and vegetables at every meal.

   _____

10. Tanya thought about the upcoming math test with <u>apprehension</u>. She knew that she would do better on the test if she faced it with calmness.

    _____

Unit 9: Building Vocabulary Through Word Meaning Clues

Activity 9-11: What I Have Learned (continued)

Complete each of the following.

11. When possible, use the _____ of your textbook to learn the meaning of an unknown word that is used in your textbook.

12. When you select the meaning of an unknown word to match the way in which the textbook writer used the word, you are using _____ .

13. Once you learn the meaning of a word, you should review the word _____ .

14. The first word meaning clue to look for is a (an) _____ clue.

15. A good way to review the meaning of a word you learned is to use the word when _____ and _____ .

Answer the following questions about the vocabulary building strategy.

16. In which step should you write a word and its meaning on the My Vocabulary Words form?

    _____

17. What is the first thing to do when using the review procedure in Step 5?

    _____

18. Why is it desirable to use the glossary of your textbook to learn the meaning of an unknown word used in your textbook?

    _____

19. Which step should you skip if a visual clue to the meaning of an unknown word is provided?

    _____

20. What should you do in Step 1?

    _____